THE ACCIDENT GAME:

CLAIMS REVIEW FOR COST CONTAINMENT IN PHYSICAL THERAPY

NATHANIEL RANDOLPH, R.P.T.
LOUIS NANNI
and LEONARD C. REDMOND, III, ESQ.

WITH

RODNEY CARLISLE, Ph.D.
CARL FASSL, M.A.

Published by
Regal Publishing Corporation

1995

Copyright © 1995 Nathaniel Randolph

Library of Congress Catalog Card Number: 94-74637
ISBN 0-936918-13-6

Regal Publishing Corporation
321 New Albany Road
Moorestown, NJ 08057

Commentary

The most unprofessional types of behavior with physical therapists and physicians are among those who play the "Accident Game," providing therapy where no therapy is needed for people who are well. In the Accident Game, the therapist knows that the patient was referred by a doctor to whom the patient was referred by an attorney. The therapist provides the six to eight weeks or more of therapy asked for by the physician and/or the attorney, for only minimal soft-tissue injuries. And that's wrong. That's unethical, that's unprofessional. It is treating beyond the actual benefit merely for the financial reward. Everybody benefits: the lawyer, the doctor, the patient, although the patient in the long run does not really benefit, because he gets the smallest piece of the action out of the Accident Game. Some doctors and physical therapists will actually lie and put things in the objective findings that were not actually there, in order to "justify" the care. Sometimes, they actually make up things, and they get caught in court when the truth comes out. They will make up objective findings. When they do that, it is just a racket.

Nathaniel Randolph

Introduction

During the 1980s, costs of medical care increased in the United States at a rate about twice that of the general inflation. Due to that factor, as well as to increased litigation, the cost of automobile insurance increased by a rate three to five times the rate for general inflation. By the mid 1980s, "rate-payers," that is, the general consumers of insurance, were in rebellion across the country. In states with initiative and referendum, anti-insurance legislation took the form of ballot propositions. In other states, legislative investigations led to a variety of reforms, including fee schedules, mandatory peer review, and expanded areas of no-fault coverage, in attempts to control the cost of bodily injury and personal injury insurance.

The Supreme Court decision of 1978 which allowed attorneys to advertise contributed to increased litigation and to higher negotiated settlements, as attorneys based their fees on the total amount recovered. Auto injury had become a gamble: with attorneys presiding over the casino, holding out hopes that the injured party could win the accident game, the recipient of a big settlement. While substantial financial awards were necessary or deserved in genuine cases of severe accident and severe pain and suffering on the part of the injured, the incentive was present for both attorneys and accident victims to escalate the cost of the injury. The incentives for the "padded" bill increased. The strains and pains which accompanied many auto injuries because of the forward-backward snap of collisions, technically called soft-tissue injuries, were particularly difficult to evaluate. How severe was the injury? How much treatment was required? The complaints in soft-tissue injury sprains and strains were difficult to prove or disprove objectively, providing opportunities for exaggeration, falsification, and a variety of deceptions.

In the United States, various health care professionals and providers deal with different aspects of soft tissue injuries. Physical therapy, with the mission of alleviating pain and restoring function, was an essential element in the care of large numbers of automobile accident victims. Some physical therapists discovered that they too, could share in the rewards of the accident game, by exaggerating the duration, frequency, cost, or necessity of their treatments. Sometimes those exaggerations occurred with the knowledge and consent of patient and attorney, in a rudimentary conspiracy to milk the insurance policy for all it was worth; in other cases, physical therapists simply attempted to maximize their own income through artificially inflating the treatment or the billing.

This book focuses on that one aspect of the automobile accident game: the problem of evaluating the legitimacy of physical therapy billings in soft-tissue injury cases sprains and strains. While this issue may at first seem to be a narrow one, concerning only a few specialists, on analysis it soon reveals itself as a set of interrelated problems, touching on several professions, and having ramifications for the whole society. The training of physical therapists centers around anatomy, kinesiology, and the practical evaluation and treatment of musculo-skeletal injury, with the objective of restoration of function. Members of this profession, however, work with others with very different training: insurance adjusters, claims reviewers, and supervisory personnel; rehabilitative social workers, hospital and clinical administrative personnel, a range of medical specialists and health care providers; attorneys, judges, and the general public, both as litigants and as juries. To understand the part that physical therapy plays in the escalating costs of health care and of auto insurance, and the abuse and over use of that health system, requires a broad look at interrelated fields.

This book is written from the background of a physical therapist, with 20 years of practical experience and over ten years experience in peer-review. I have evaluated hundreds of claims, and have testified and given depositions in scores of cases, evaluating the legitimacy of accident claims in the physical therapy area. I have been appalled at some of the abuses which I have encountered, perpetrated by unscrupulous practitioners. While the vast majority of both health care workers and attorneys adhere to decent ethical standards, the repeated attempts of a small proportion of both groups to "cheat the system" represent a large contribution to the escalation of health care costs and automobile insurance premiums over the 1990s. As a member of the American Physcial Therapy Association and as an appointed member of a State Licencing Board, I have worked to establish standards which would clarify the gray areas and which would insure ethical practice. At times the battle is discouraging. The lure of easy money, the combined factors of greed, corporate inertia, the massive scale of fraudulent claims, and the multitude of state laws and regulations, have all stood as barriers to reform in this area.

As the work mounted, I concluded that I should present my conclusions and analysis to a wider audience. I have also decided to include my frank opinions, particularly about those aspects of the system which I feel are most outrageous.

I worked with Dr. Rodney Carlisle, and his assistant, Carl Fassl, in researching and writing this work. My goal was to bring in experienced writers and generalists, and to present the issues to them, so that my observations and experience could be organized and presented to others. In a series of tape recorded sessions, we discussed various aspects of the issue. They have captured both my analysis and my opinions in the following work. To assist the reader, we have worked to separate fact and opinion, and have set the opinions off from the main body of the text in specially- designated editorial comments. In the body of the work I have attempted to provide a variety of information for those who are striving for cost- containment in the area of physical therapy. To the insurance claims review people, I have spelled out what physical therapy is, how it should be practiced, and the sorts of abuses frequently encountered in some claims. I have also described the sorts of documentation the therapist should maintain, and the specific procedures which an insurance claims reviewer or adjuster can adopt to initiate a sensible system of claims review to identify cases of waste, fraud, or abuse. Insurance adjusters need a set of practical checklists, like those they use to insure coverage and to guarantee the type of coverage, for the screening of the legitimate from the suspect cases. Drafts of those checklists are included. Lists of commonly used abbreviations, standards of treatment in physical therapy cases, and other technical information are presented in a series of appendices at the end of the book.

I have also provided background which will put the problem in its larger context of insurance costs, automobile liability law, and courtroom practice. That background should help the general reader, including the attorneys, judges, and juries who must think through these issues on a case by case basis. Hopefully, it may also serve to inform state legislators, insurance commission members, and their staffs who are engaged in modifying the regulations and laws governing insurance and health care practices.

This work includes descriptions of physical therapy practices presented in non-technical language for the general reader, rather than as a detailed explanation for those studying how to provide therapy. As in many fields, the jargon and terminology developed within a field tends to clarify and facilitate communication within the field; unfortunately, specialized language tends to exclude non-specialists from understanding. In this work, I have attempted to provide background, definitions, and basic information, to help bridge the inter-disciplinary gaps.

When properly applied, the guidelines in this work should help in distinguishing the legitimate claim from a problem claim. The guidelines will aid in recognizing the proper use of physical therapy for the rehabilitation of soft tissue injuries, will help to identify billing irregularities, and will help to better determine if care was unnecessary or unreasonable.

My objective is to make the book a useful text or handbook for insurance personnel, and at the same time, to provide to others concerned with limiting the costs which spring from the abuses of the accident game, a deeper understanding of the issues and problems. I have attempted to be brief and to the point, and at the same time, to provide definitions for concepts and ideas which may be familiar to specialists in the different pertinent disciplines. I have also included a few anecdotal examples of the sorts of abuses encountered for illustrative purposes, but have tried to avoid burdening the reader with excessive numbers of notional "case histories." My hope is that this work will contribute, in some small way, to the current national effort to rein in these costs and to control unethical practices which have contributed to the problem.

I belong to a growing informal and loose network of individuals, working in utilization review, in peer review, in the insurance business, and before the bar, who have dedicated ourselves to establishing the "Sentinel Effect." We believe that setting up a fair and equitable system which rejects the payment of inappropriate or unethical charges will produce a reduction in the submission of such charges. Proper utilization review and claims investigation resulting in the denial of payment for unreasonable or unnecessary care and the exposure of those who betray their trust, should in the long run make a contribution to controlling insurance costs. It will also represent a small, but important, contribution to the wider cause of social justice.

Louis Nanni served as co-author on the first six chapters of the work, working closely with me in developing the thinking and in editing the manuscript. Chapter six is largely based on material provided by Leonard Redman, Esquire, of Baltimore, Maryland, who has done much to inform the insurance industry of cost-containment strategies from a legal perspective.

Nathaniel Randolph
Washington, D.C.
1995

CONTENTS

Chapter One   Physical Therapy: The Profession and Professional Treatment 1

Chapter Two   Over Utilization of Physical Therapy 21

Chapter Three The Insurance Business: Cost Containment and Utilization Review 41

Chapter Four   Documentation. 57

Chapter Five   The Claims Review Process 75

Chapter Six   The Role of the Attorney in Cost Containment. 93

Appendices

1. Physical Therapy Guidelines 109
2. Abbreviations in common use 115
3. CPT Codes 119
4. Normal Range of Motion, in Degrees 125
5. Physical Therapy Modalities 126

1 Physical Therapy

THE PROFESSION AND PROFESSIONAL TREATMENT

The Profession
The Practice
Evaluation
The "SOAP" Format
Treatment
Techniques and Modalities
Tens
A Professional Treatment Program
Professionalism

THE PROFESSION OF PHYSICAL THERAPY

Physical therapy is just what the term implies: the application of **physical** agents such as heat, ultrasound, massage, therapeutic exercise, or electrical stimulation for therapeutic purposes. Physical therapy is useful in the treatment of musculoskeletal injuries, to establish the functional rehabilitation of the patient recovering from an illness or an accident. The correct practice of physical therapy of course involves more than just the application of the physical agents, or the "modalities," to the patient. That application must be part of a systematic approach that involves examination and evaluation of the patient, assessment of the problem, and the planning of treatment. Furthermore, the treatment must be continually assessed and modified if required. In addition, the physical therapist is responsible for educating patients to deal with their disabilities and with the functional rehabilitation of the body.

A distinction can be drawn between the professional's approach and the technician's approach to physical therapy. The professional expects to conduct the evaluation of the patient, assess the patient's problems, make judgments as to the propriety of treatment, and to adjust the treatment plan in response to changed conditions or improvements on the patient's part. The technician or assistant applies the physical therapy modalities, leaving the questions of judgment to the physical therapist. State laws recognize this distinction, by licensing registered physical therapists and physicians to conduct evaluations and to modify treatment plans, while only permitting physical therapist aides or assistants to administer the modalities. However, many Registered or Licensed Physical Therapists take the technical approach, rather than the professional one, and operate only by prescription or order from physicians. Most states license osteopaths, dentists, podiatrists, nurse practitioners and chiropractors in addition to physicians to provide orders and prescriptions to physical therapists.

> *Commentary*
>
> *A lot of physical therapists are operating as technicians. When do you decide when the patient has had enough treatment? A professional has to be able to make his own judgment, not just when the doctor says so. But some act as highly paid technicians. Some come out of school, just apply modalities, only putting on hot packs, making in excess of fifty thousand a year... so the cost of care skyrockets. Furthermore, often when excessive care is denied in utilization review, a PT will write in and to say that they did the treatment because "the doctor ordered it."*
>
> *Nathaniel Randolph*

There are a range of possibly appropriate treatments for every condition, and one professional physical therapist might choose one treatment, where another would choose quite a different procedure. Physical therapy is an eclectic and evolving field. Some specialists will use only one or two modalities, or use hands-on mobilization techniques only, whereas others have been trained in and accept a wide variety of modalities. There are a variety of schools of thought for each condition, and research to determine the best methodology is lacking. This is the nature of the profession and is not a legitimate reason to doubt or deny claims. As long as the modalities are not redundant, are appropriate to the condition, and are among those that are legally approved for use by physical therapists, their use is generally legitimate. For example, a preference by one therapist for one type of superficial heat treatment over an alternate preferred by some others in the profession would not constitute grounds for questioning a claim. Such choices would fall within the range of professional decisions.

The range of modalities open to use by physical therapists is governed by the laws of the state in which they practice, and is constantly being expanded with the advent of new technologies and procedures. By the 1990s, most states included the following in their definition of the types of physical treatment which could be applied by physical therapists in a variety of different forms:

heat or cold
therapeutic exercise
electricity

mobilization manual techniques
therapeutic massage
air, light, or water
ultra sound

In addition, physical therapists are licensed to perform "non-invasive" tests of neuromuscular functions to aid in the detection of problems or in planning treatment or its modification. Such tests include measures of range of motion and strength, reaction to pressure or touch, but exclude x-rays or tests which require drawing of blood or other fluids -- the "invasive" techniques. Most states prohibit performance of EMG by Physical Therapist.

The training of physical therapists usually consists of a four-year college course, with concentration in the sciences and particularly in physiology, anatomy, kinesiology and in advanced courses in the practical application of techniques and modalities in treatment situations. During the final two years, there is often a clinical affiliation, in which the student spends time actually working in a hospital or other clinical settings. Physical therapist have graduated with a Bachelor of Science degree, with a certificate in physical therapy. There are some certificate programs where people who already have training in a related field can obtain the certificate in a one-year or two year program. Some schools are beginning to offer a five year or six year MS program, which usually is more research-oriented. In addition to the training, state licensing boards require that physical therapists take a national licensing examination, given on the same day nationwide, three times a year.

The primary professional association of physical therapists in the United States, the American Physical Therapy Association, gathers and frequently updates information on the number of physical therapists in the United States, their income levels, their demographics, and the nature of the settings in which they practice. The association identifies trends and developments in the profession, keeps its members informed, decides on reforms and policies pertinent to the profession, and assists state associations in lobbying efforts to modify state laws and Federal regulations.

Based upon surveys of membership, in 1987, about 75 per cent of the members of the association were women, about 25 percent men. The percentage of women had grown slightly over the period 1978-1987.[1] In 1987, over 95 per cent of the Association were Caucasian. About 30 per cent of the members of the Association had been physical therapists for less than six years, and over half had been in the profession for less than eleven years. These statistics do not apply directly to the whole profession, because less than half of all registered physical therapists are members of the association. The Association noted that physical therapists are licensed to practice in 50 states, the District of Columbia, and Puerto Rico, and that the number of physical therapists for each 10,000 members of the population runs from about 1 to about 4 in most states. Several states had much higher proportions. Vermont, Connecticut, Maryland, and New Hampshire, all reported more than six physical therapists per 10,000. In most states, the number of physical therapists had increased over the 1980s, and by 1988, there were about 90,000 physical therapists licensed to practice in the United States, up from about 51,000 in 1983.[2]

Several conclusions and implications can be drawn from the raw figures. The profession grew drastically in the 1980s, with most of the addition coming from young graduates entering the profession. One factor causing the expansion of the profession was the presence of relatively high beginning salaries, and relatively high incomes after a few years of service, for individuals with four years of college training. The full time salaried physical therapist in 1986 had a mean income of $32,000, and the full time self-employed therapist had a mean income of nearly $73,000. As in most professions, there was a gender gap in income, with men earning more than women. However, for both men and women, the salaries were quite high compared to others with 4-year baccalaureate degrees. Considering only those with 8 or less years of experience working in salaried settings, women earned a median $27,000, and men a median $32,000. Self employed and more senior therapists did much better, with self-employed males with over 9 years experience showing a median income over $100,000.

The statistics suggest a number of points, but certainly indicate that through the mid-1980s, the profession was a "hot ticket" for those seeking immediate good incomes and prospects for high incomes after a four-year college program.

Commentary
Part of the problem with greed in our profession is that too many people have entered physical therapy only to make a buck. A professional attitude has to put the patient and the patient's needs first. Our code of ethics says that. But you have to remember that for a lot of the younger kids, the main reason they went into physical therapy is that they read somewhere that you could make good money, not that they wanted to help people. That's wrong, and we have to do a lot of education and a lot of work in the profession to get it right.
Nathaniel Randolph

Since physical therapy is regulated by state laws, there is considerable variation from state to state as to exactly what a therapist is allowed to do. As of January, 1990, 41 states allowed physical therapists to conduct an initial evaluation of a patient without referral from a physician. Twenty four of those states also allowed the physical therapist to begin treatment of a patient without referral. Most of the laws allowing this practice of "Direct Access" had been passed in the 1980s, with only 2 of the 24 states permitting direct access under older laws.[3]

> *Commentary*
> *You have contract situations in hospitals, where they can't get enough PTs -- in some cases the therapists quit and then come back to the hospital at an increased fee through a contract company. He will come back making almost twice as much in the contract situation. The hospital's cost is far higher in that way. That is a big problem today in physical therapy. Some hospitals are desperate for physical therapists. The shortage is due in large part to the increase in the ustilization, as much as in the need for physical therapy.*
>
> *Nathaniel Randolph*

In general, the state associations of physical therapists advocated direct access, as did the national APTA, and cited the fact that the United States Army allowed treatment by physical therapists without referral. As the movement gained ground, state associations would point to the legitimacy of direct access in those states which had already allowed it. Thus, for example, in 1983, the association in Arizona pointed to the fact that laws in California, Maryland, Nebraska and Massachusetts already permitted direct access. The growth of the movement was cited as evidence that the movement was appropriate. The addition of each state to the list of those allowing direct access was duly noted in the lobbying efforts of those state associations still trying to achieve the reform.

In the state of Colorado, the Physical Therapy Association hired a lobbying firm to assist in securing passage of direct access legislation in 1988. The Minnesota group hired a survey firm, and relied on "grass roots" lobbying by physical therapists themselves. The groups in both states succeeded in arranging for full direct access.

TABLE
States that deny full direct access* as of 1994:

ALABAMA	OHIO
ARKANSAS	OREGON
DELAWARE	PUERTO RICO
INDIANA	SOUTH CAROLINA
MISSOURI	VIRGINIA
	VIRGIN ISLANDS

* These states require patients to seek the services of physical therapists, including treatment, only with referral from a physician or other health care professional. All others allow some form of direct access for evaluation and treatment or evaluation only.

Source: APTA

The national APTA supported the state associations in this effort, and provided lobbying and supporting materials for activists in the remaining states. The APTA's position regarding direct access was that the "phenomenon" of requiring physician referral "is especially misguided in its application to physical therapists. No other health profession has patient access to its services so severely limited, and few other health professionals are so demonstrably well qualified for practice without referral."[5]

Further, the associations argued that physicians usually relied, even where referral was required, upon the judgment of the physical therapists as to the nature of pain, its cause, and the appropriate modality or treatment to be applied. Since physician referral was often pro forma, the associations argued, it served little purpose. Physical therapists were qualified by training, experience, and by constant concern with the specialized nature of problems related to pain and rehabilitation to provide examination, diagnosis, and plan of treatment. The associations pointed out that liability for malpractice or claims against physical therapists had not increased in those states providing direct access, and that therefore, one should not expect the cost of physical therapy to climb due to increased premiums for malpractice insurance.[6]

Not everyone in the profession agreed with the principle of direct access, however, or with advocates who argued that it should be extended to other states. Requiring referral from physicians has several built-in protections for the patient, and could serve to protect the public to some extent from unscrupulous or unethical practice of the profession for profit alone. However, even where physician referral is required, abuses of the insurance system and over-use of physical therapy is common, sometimes with collusion by the physicians, and sometimes without. The rapid growth of the profession, and the prevalence of young and relatively less experienced practitioners in many areas is another argument for going slowly in the expansion of direct access.

The list of states allowing direct access is subject to change. In general, one might expect the legislation to allow more states permitting examination without referral, and a gradual increase in states permitting treatment without referral through the 1990s. Insurance professionals should keep informed of changes in their particular states, and with changes in the practice of the health professions more generally.

One particular form of ethical abuse which the APTA has urged its members to watch out for and to avoid, is "referral for profit." This is the technical term for any arrangement in which the referring physician or other practitioner refers a patient to another practitioner and receives financial compensation as a result of the referral. The practice is popularly known as a "kickback."

In some jurisdictions, referral for profit can very readily occur, and it can lead to gray-area ethical concerns. Frequently physical therapists or physical therapy assistants work under an agreement with or are employed directly by referring practitioners or organizations. In these situations, the referring practitioner can profit directly from the referral. The APTA believes that these situations offer serious potential for abuse, and recommend that existing statutes be amended at the state level to prohibit such arrangements.[7]

Another area of referral for profit occurs with Physician- Owned Physical Therapy clinics or "POPTs". The APTA points out that in the case of physician-owned clinics or other situations in which a physical therapist is in the direct or indirect employ of a referring practitioner, "The potential for patient abuse in these arrangements is high." There is "a significantly increased incentive to refer patients for physical therapy when such services are not needed." The range, duration, and number of treatments might be increased, and patients are deprived of the freedom of choice of the practitioner who might best serve their needs.

In 1983, the APTA House of Delegates identified the referral for profit problem and began a campaign against it. The APTA traced the growth of POPTs to economic incentives, often justified by arguments citing increased physician productivity and cost-savings to the medical care consumer. The APTA identified various arrangements which could create the dubious ethical situation of referral for profit in addition to POPTs, including direct employment, rebates for referrals, and rental of office space by physicians to therapists, often at a higher price than equivalent space elsewhere. Those situations were identified as likely to produce over-utilization of services, increased cost to insurance companies or other "third party" payers, and non- medical profits to the physician. For all of these reasons, the APTA campaigned against referral for profit arrangements and lobbied for changes in legislation after 1983.

> *Commentary*
>
> *You see cases of physician-owned clinics, and/or lawyer-owned clinics. The laws prevent physicians owning pharmacies and referring their business there, and they are strict about that. The states should clamp down on physician owned clinics and these arrangements with attorneys. Sometimes it's disgusting. You know it is just a racket, with the lawyer, the doctor, and the PT all out to rack up a profit. I have reviewed hundreds of cases where the physical therapist provided extraordinary amounts of care only to enhance the personal injury case.*
>
> *Nathaniel Randolph*

Physicians resisted attempts to limit their right to invest in physical therapy clinics. One compromise arrangement was worked out in Virginia in 1986 legislation, which required financial disclosure by physicians to the patient of any interest held by the physician in any facility to which the patient was referred.[8] Florida and Arizona passed similar laws, while Missouri simply outlawed the practice of physicians hiring physical therapists or investing in physical therapy clinics.[9]

Congressman Fortney Stark of California led an effort to outlaw medicare payments in cases of referral for profit. In this area, as in others in this rapidly changing field, insurance professionals need to keep informed on changes in both state and federal law, and be aware of cases of referral for profit. Particularly in those states which allow referral for profit, or which allow POPTs, the insurance professional should be particularly alert to the likelihood of the abuse of over- utilization. Patterns of over-utilization of physical therapy are more prevalent where the profit-motive of referral adds to the likelihood that the patient will receive unnecessary or excessively long treatment.

One could view the effort to increase the practice of direct access as a means of combatting referral for profit. Clearly, in those states in which a patient can choose a therapist and begin treatment without referral by a physician, the amount of referral for profit from physician to physical therapist is likely to be lower. On the other hand, direct access can readily lead to other conflict of interest abuses, as physical therapists seek to increase their business through non-medical referrals, such as those by attorneys. They might also arrange to provide unnecessary referrals from the physical therapist to other professionals, with a rebate or other understanding. Such practices are obviously not in the patient's interest. While complete independence in the form of direct access avoids some of the problem of conflict of interest generated in the POPT and the joint-venture modes of referral-for-profit, independence can also foster ethical problems of its own.

> *Commentary*
> *You have doctors in joint ventures with lawyers, and even situations where attorneys own clinics--all to take advantage of the soft-tissue injury market. Everyone wants a piece of that soft-tissue market generated by workmen's compensation and auto injury. Basically it is greed. It is fast money.*
> *— Nathaniel Randolph*

THE PRACTICE OF PHYSICAL THERAPY

The field of physical therapy is constantly subject to change not only with respect to legislation, but also as the result of research and the development of new equipment, new techniques, and new modalities. Nevertheless, the education received by physical therapists is very explicit in setting guidelines for the correct assessment, evaluation, treatment, recording, and treatment of patients. Non-medical professionals in claims review situations need to be familiar with the basic standards of good practice in physical therapy in order to evaluate insurance claims. This section is intended to provide a general background on the nature of correct physical therapy practice, to spell out the areas of judgment and performance which are usually left to the physical therapist, and to indicate the sorts of evaluation techniques and treatment modalities usually employed by physical therapists.

EVALUATION

Evaluation is an ongoing process, involving a complete initial examination, which is essential. Any effective treatment plan depends upon the initial examination. The selection of the appropriate treatment techniques depends upon the complete evaluation of the patient. There is a wide range of different tests, measurements and sequences of procedures used for evaluating the patient and collecting the data. Several accepted methods of evaluation are constantly being taught, but all essentially require thoroughness and accuracy.

Data collected during the initial evaluation of a patient should be relevant, accurate and measurable, and the data should be recorded as objectively as possible. It should be in a format easily interpreted by other health care professionals. Findings from the initial examination guide the therapist in the selection of appropriate treatment techniques. Initial evaluation does not provide all the answers to what sort of treatment may be required or how it may be necessary to modify that treatment. Using the principles of science, the first evaluation and the first trial treatment should be regarded as a test of an hypothesis. After the trial treatment is performed, the patient should be assessed to determine whether the nature of the treatment program should be modified. The patient must be rechecked during the course of treatment to determine progress, and an on-going evaluation and assessment of the patient must be maintained. That on-going evaluation and assessment should form the basis of any future modification of the treatment plan.

The only exception to the rule of a complete evaluation and assessment of the patient's status during the initial evaluation is in the case of severe or acute pain or discomfort which should be clearly documented. For example, when therapists suspect a fracture, they immediately refer the patient to an orthopedic surgeon or other specialist. A licensed physician must first determine if the problem is musculoskeletal, and must rule out the possibility that the pain results from fracture or dislocation or other medical condition. In the event of acute pain on the initial visit, the therapist should take a complete history of the problem, and if that history does not contraindicate the findings, the therapist may proceed to treat the patient's problem. In those 42 states which allow direct access by patients to physical therapists, without referrals from physicians, it is even more incumbent upon the physical therapist to be certain in the evaluation and diagnosis whether to proceed. If there is any doubt, the therapist may need to seek further evaluation from another professional. Physical therapists have sufficient training to know when they need further professional opinion, and seeking it is often appropriate. After the symptoms subside, the therapist must then go ahead and carry out a complete evaluation. The explicit goal of the initial evaluation is to determine the patient's problem. Subjective questioning and objective tests should be individualized to the particular situation to maximize the information obtained.

THE "SOAP" FORMAT

The acronym SOAP, standing for Subjective, Objective, Assessment, and Plan, is commonly used in many clinical settings to describe both the process of, and the recording of, the evaluation. The record of such an examination is sometimes called a set of "SOAP Notes." Although the SOAP format is widely used, not all health professionals us it. Many write in narrative form, but their notes should contain the same sorts of information and the same essential elements.

In the Subjective section, the practitioner discusses with the patient's own perception of the symptoms. The practitioner learns the patient's complaints and tries, through specific questions to get an accurate description of several different aspects of the patient's symptoms. In particular, the practitioner wants to find out the behavior of the symptoms: how they are aggravated. That is, are they more severe during sitting, or standing, or during a particular activity or motion? Further, the specific location of the symptoms should be determined, together with the time or date of the onset of the symptoms and their course and duration. The practitioner should also determine from the patient any effects of previous treatment. The practitioner should find out the details of any related medical problems in the patient's past. Because all of this information is determined from the patient, it is regarded as subjective; nevertheless, every attempt is made to put the questions and to record the answers in as specific and as accurate a manner as possible.

While the Subjective portion of the procedure concerns itself with **symptoms**, the Objective portion concerns itself with **signs**. The objective physical examination is the actual observation of physical condition and performance during tests and diagnostic procedures used to evaluate the patient's condition. The initial screening will determine the exact location of the disorder. The patient may complain of a general pain in the neck and back, and the therapist will make every effort to locate the specific area. The examination can also include vital signs, such as temperature, heart rate and blood pressure. It should also include the therapist's general observations and visual inspection of the patient. There should be a posture and gait analysis, and a measurement of leg lengths when indicated. In order to rule out associated injuries, the therapist also conducts tests such as palpation, tests of blood circulation, and neurological testing to determine if there has been neurological involvement. This is done through determining if the patient is sensitive to touch in affected areas, and through tests of reflexes and balance.

To determine the extent of joint or muscle involvement, the therapist will conduct tests of "range of motion" of the joints. The therapist will conduct tests of mobility and flexibility of muscles and ligaments, and will test the patient's strength with manual muscle testing. Activities of daily living (often abbreviated "ADL"), such as tying shoes, picking up objects, opening doors, and other similar motions will be tested and recorded. "Anthropometric" measurements will also be made, recording specifics about the patient's girth, circumference of thigh, neck, and wrists.

In recording the "SOAP Notes," the distinction between subjective comments by the patient, and objective findings of the therapist should be obvious. In general, the subjective comments about symptoms, although they may be specific, are taken on faith from the patient. In general, the objective comments recorded by therapists are the reproducible results of their own observations, tests and measurements, and are recorded in numerical or other verifiable form. The essence of an objective observation is that another therapist would determine and record the same fact with almost precisely the same notation. Claims adjusters and reviewers will especially note that cases of "SOAP" notes, taken on the same patient by different practitioners, should show similar subjective remarks by the patient and similar findings of objective conditions. Wide discrepancies between the SOAP notes on the same patient can be an indication of a problem on a claim and suggest the need for closer review.

The "Assessment" section of the SOAP procedure consists in listing the problems found in both the subjective and the objective examination, and it will also list the short term and the long term treatment goals. The Assessment will include an identification of major problems. It can include a statement of impressions and a notation of tentative or firm conclusions drawn.

The "Plan" in the SOAP procedure, is of course the crucial outcome of the whole process. It should consist of an outline of the treatment planned, including its frequency and duration. Any specific plans as to patient and family education should be included, as well as plans for short term and long term follow- up. The Plan should also include the patient's reaction to the first treatment.

The evaluation process is ongoing, and it is expanded each time the patient is seen. Reassessment should continue and treatment modifications should be made as necessary. The therapist continually assesses the effectiveness of the treatment and does not conclude the assessment process until the patient's problems are resolved.

TREATMENT

The treatment programs should be developed specifically for each patient condition, and should be based on the results of the initial evaluation or subsequent evaluations. A so-called "shotgun" approach to treating the patient with a wide variety of modalities, hoping that something will work, is inappropriate. Such an approach has no place in a sound, problem-oriented treatment program. Not only is it difficult to properly evaluate the effectiveness of any particular treatment, such an approach usually leads to increased costs, clinical and equipment utilization time, and unnecessary exposure of the patient to multiple modalities.

For these reasons, a sensible, planned treatment approach should be based on a clear evaluation, a set of stated goals, and a sensibly-chosen set of modalities or treatment procedures. For the claims adjuster or other insurance professional reviewing the physical therapy record of the patient's examination and treatment, the logical connection from evaluation to treatment may be obvious. In correct procedure, the interpretation of information obtained from the evaluation of the patient forms the basis of the treatment selection and the treatment plan.

The goals which derive from the evaluation may be divided into short-range and long-range objectives. Among the short term goals, the physical therapist might need to protect the involved area, decrease the activity level, increase the range of motion, and allow for rest, decrease pain, and decrease inflammation. If pain is the dominant limiting factor, which it often is in the sorts of musculoskeletal problems arising from accidents which generate disputed claims, the focus of treatment should begin with reducing pain and spasm, protecting the part, and returning the patient's normal posture, strength, and mobility.

Long term goals should also be explicit. Legitimate long term goals for physical therapy include the following: increased musculotendinous flexibility, increased muscle strength or "muscle power", increased endurance, and the maintenance of cardiovascular endurance. The therapist may list as a long term goal the restoration of a specific normal biomechanical function. Clearly, a general goal in most physical therapy is to return the patient to previous functional activity.

TECHNIQUES AND MODALITIES IN PHYSICAL THERAPY

The physical therapist requires professional training to employ modalities and procedures, which, if applied incorrectly, could worsen the condition, or endanger the patient. However, several techniques and devices can play a legitimate role in treating a patient's symptoms in a manner that will avoid any risk of exacerbation of the symptoms. Many of these sorts of low- risk techniques can be applied or used by the patient with a minimum amount of familiarization or training, and do not necessarily require constant supervision by a trained physical therapist. The range of modalities of treatment which the patient can proceed with by himself or herself after an introduction or brief training include:

Range of Modalities Utilized by Patient
(after brief introduction or training)

Assistive Devices:	Flexibility Exercises:	Palliative Heat:
crutches, canes, taping and wrapping	range of motion	some superficial heat modalities such as electric heating pads

The Range of Modalities Utilized by Trained Physical Therapists

Superficial heat	Deep heat	Cold or Cryothermy.	Electro therapy:	Massage	Traction	Exercise:
whirlpools, hydrocollator packs (or "hot packs"), moist air, hot paraffin, ultraviolet light, and topical counter-irritants.	ultra sound, short wave diathermy, microwave diathermy, phonophoresis combined ultrasound and medication.	Spray and stretch, ice packs, and ice massage.	low volt therapy, high-voltage galvanic therapy, TENS units, Iontophoresis.	manual mechanical	cervical pelvic manual	four modes: passive, active-assistive, active, resistive; three types: isometric, isotonic, isokinetic.

A trained physical therapist uses professional judgment in incorporating various modalities into a treatment plan. The insurance professional should have some idea of when certain modalities are appropriate, and when they are inappropriate or "contraindicated," so that claims that appear to be based on inappropriate treatment can be subjected to more senior review. The following discussion is intended to provide to the non-professional a general sense of the purpose of the various modalities.

Superficial heat and cold are both popular treatments for soft tissue injuries or dysfunctions. Heat, or "thermotherapy" takes several forms, including hot packs, hot baths, moist warm towels, water bottles, infrared lamps or whirlpool treatments. Heat is traditionally used to treat subacute and chronic pain and muscle spasm. It is often used to produce a local, or topical effect. The effects of heat are vasodilation and erythema, that is, an increased blood flow and reddening of the skin. Heat produces relief of pain, and decreases the sensation of slow nerve fibers. Heat also produces decreased electrical resistance in the skin. In general, heat has a sedative effect, and produces a superficial muscle relaxation. It is used adjunctively to prepare for exercise or traction, and is often used prior to ultrasound or electrical stimulation. The general indications for the use of heat are that it provides pain relief, decreases joint stiffness, increases the extensibility of collagen tissue, relieves muscle spasm, increases blood flow, and assists in the resolution of inflammatory infiltrates, edema or exudates. Heat is not indicated as a treatment for tissues that have inadequate blood supply, in cases of malignancy, or where there are sensation problems. And in general, heat should not be applied in cases of swelling.

As already mentioned, a number of superficial heat treatments for palliative purposes can be employed by patients themselves; application of superficial heat by a therapist in a clinic simply for palliative purposes without it being part of a treatment plan or program aimed at rehabilitation is incorrect utilization of the skills of the therapist. Insurance claims for such treatment are frequently denied, as the patient is not engaged in rehabilitation, but is simply receiving a treatment to temporarily feel better, which could be done at home rather than in a clinical setting.

Commentary
If a modality has not worked within six to eight weeks, it probably won't, and some other treatment should be considered. If the patient is coming in to do simple unsupervised exercises and to receive hotpacks and ultrasound, when he can apply heat at home, he does not need to come in. Are the skills of a physical therapist required? Is a therapist necessary, or is it maintenance or palliative care? Is it requiring the skills of a therapist or only a technician, one who just puts on the heating packs?

Nathaniel Randolph

Superficial heat, of course, does have a part in clinical settings, where it is part of the rehabilitation program. Superficial heating modalities include hot packs, hot paraffin, and whirlpool, which are moist-heat and heat lamps (infrared) which are dry heat. Hot packs or hydrocollator packs are usually applied with toweling to protect the skin, with the temperature of the pack in the range of 180 degrees Fahrenheit, but with the toweling preventing the temperature at the skin from exceeding the "tolerance level" of about 111 degrees Fahrenheit. The packs cool off and need renewing after about 20 to 30 minutes. Superficial heat is "adjunctive," that is it is usually used in conjunction with other treatment such as ultrasound, electrical stimulation, or to prepare an area for exercise.[10]

Paraffin is kept melted in a bath, and is applied at a temperature of 118 to 126 degrees Fahrenheit. It is particularly useful for hands or feet, because of their uneven surfaces, and the need to penetrate evenly. It is often used for mobilizing stiff hands or stiff feet prior to exercise.[11]

Cold or cryotherapy is used in acute painful conditions, usually in the first 24 to 36 hours after an injury, when there is any amount of swelling present. However, it is not necessarily wrong to apply cold later in a treatment program as some patients respond well to cold. The local topic effects of cold are vasoconstriction, or decreasing the blood flow. It is used to decrease swelling, to reduce pain and spasm, to reduce inflammation, and it has an anesthetic effect. It is most effective in reducing spasm in acute stages. It can be applied by ice bag, by ice pack, or by ice massage.

Deep heating modalities include several methods. Short wave diathermy uses electromagnetic radiation. It can be very effective, and is used in large body parts such as the back, thigh, or hip. It heats subcutaneous tissues and muscles. Microwave diathermy can penetrate deeper and can be more focussed on a localized area. In general, diathermy techniques are not as popular in the 1990s as they were in the past. The effects of deep heating modalities are that they: increase the extensibility of collagen tissues, decrease joint stiffness, relieve pain, relieve muscle spasm, assist in the resolution of inflammatory infiltrates, and increase blood flow. Deep heat is indicated for ligamentous strains and sprains, muscle spasm, joint stiffness and contractions, capsule lesions, degenerative joint disease, myofascial pain syndrome, bursitis, and synovitis. Diathermy is not indicated, and is in fact dangerous, in cases of pregnancy, or use near eyes, testes, fluid filled joints, acutely inflamed tissues, or in tissue with sensory impairment. It should not be used with patients with pacemakers, or with internal or external metallic braces or implants. The duration of a heat treatment with short wave or microwave is determined empirically, and is usually about 20 minutes to 30 minutes.[12]

Ultrasound is the most commonly used modality in treating musculoskeletal pain, after the hot pack. The ultrasound is actually a form of mechanical therapy. A crystal in the transducer or sound head vibrates in response to electrical current and produces sound waves. The sound waves cause the tissues to vibrate, thus generating heat. The ultrasound device requires a transmission medium, either a gel, an oil, or through a water bath. Ultrasound is used to reach deep tissues such as deep muscles and joint capsules. The depth of penetration of ultrasound can be up to five centimeters.[13] Ultrasound has been found to increase the extensibility of tendons, ligaments and joint capsules. It decreases inflammation and pain spasm, breaks down adhesions and calcium deposits. It also alters the conduction velocity of the nerves. The mechanical effects of ultrasound are in effect a form of micromassage or vibration of tissue. Such micromassage is excellent for reducing muscle spasm and tightness. Again, ultrasound is not indicated in cases of pregnancy or in patients with pacemakers. It should not be used over the eyes, or directly over the spinal cord after a laminectomy. It is also contraindicated in cases of malignancy, or bony growth plates in children. A sound head must be kept moving, otherwise it may cause excessive heat build-up. The application of ultrasound should avoid bony areas. Short wave diathermy can be applied around joints because it is applied with a flexible wrap, whereas microwave diathermy is applied with the radiant head positioned a few inches away from the body, and thus can only penetrate one side of the injured part. Microwave has been found particularly useful in the reduction of lower back pain, and in post-traumatic pains.[14] Microwave therapy is particularly contraindicated where edema or other gathering of fluid is present, as the fluid will increase in temperature faster than the surrounding tissue, and damage can result.[15]

In general, both short wave and microwave therapy are contraindicated in the same sorts of conditions: around tissues with fluids, over wet dressings or adhesive tape, over growing bone, over metallic implants, over the testes, around areas with hemorrhage or to people with bleeding tendency, over malignant tissue, in cases of pregnancy or tuberculosis, right after trauma when sprains or contusions are still present, or in the very young or very old. For both microwave and short wave, serious hazards arise with both internal and external metallic objects, and in individuals with pacemakers.[16]

Phonophoresis is a method of driving medication into the tissues with ultrasound, usually a topical cream containing hydrocortisone, lidocaine, or aspirin. Research has indicated that cortisol can be driven as deep as 6 centimeters into tissue with ultrasound. Further research in the area will reveal more about exactly how the process works, but researchers assume that ultrasound increases the permeability of tissues. It appears that the medication follows the direction of the sound beam, and treatments twice a week seem to improve penetration of decadron- lidocaine solutions.[17]

Ultrasound is perhaps the best way to apply heat deep inside tissues, such as in hip joints. Ultrasound has better penetration with less effect on the superficial tissue than microwave diathermy. In fact, microwave or short wave diathermy might produce skin burns without heating the interior of the hip, whereas the ultrasound modality would raise hip temperatures without affecting the surface. Ultrasound is also much safer than microwave or short wave diathermy in cases where the patient has surgical metal implants such as pins or "nails."[18]

Traction is the application of an external force to a joint or to a series of joints to cause a separation of the joint space. Cervical and lumbar, or pelvic traction are concerned with the treatment of the spinal column. In general, there are three types of traction: manual, constant, or intermittent. In manual traction, the therapist applies the force directly with his hands by pulling. Constant traction uses weight or mechanical equipment to apply a continuous stretch or pull, often on a table which some patients think resembles the medieval torture rack. Intermittent traction is applied mechanically, with gradual pulling and relaxation. In some cases, intermittent traction is the most effective because it is better tolerated than continuous traction. Intermittent traction relieves muscle spasm and pain, it relieves pressure on nerve roots as they exit the intervertebral spaces, it widens the disc spaces which have been narrowed by disc degeneration or arthritis. Traction can be used to reduce swelling and to promote circulation and to prevent the formation of adhesions.

In one sense, exercise is the most important area of emphasis for any rehabilitation program. In physical therapy treatment, the focus of exercise is on specific muscle groups or joints and on the areas of dysfunction, not on a general muscle- building, weight control, or cardiovascular endurance program common in popular self-exercise programs. Exercise can be passive, active- assisted, active, or resistive. Each of these "modes" of exercise has its own purpose. Passive exercise is directed by the therapist. The body part is carried through the range of motion. It is usually used early in the planned program to prevent tightening up, or the formation of adhesions or degenerative changes in the soft tissues, and to promote healing. Early exercise is often directed at preventing loss of range of motion. Active assistive exercise is most commonly used during post- surgical or post-traumatic situations. The patient is too limited by weakness or inhibited by pain, and is therefore assisted in the exercise by the therapist. Sometimes the assistance is simply to neutralize the effect of gravity. Exercise is contraindicated when a patient's condition is not stabilized. After a fracture or a major operation like a hip replacement, exercise which might dislodge the joint is avoided. Particularly in cases where immobilization is the treatment of choice, as in certain knee injuries, exercise is contraindicated.

Active exercise is used to maintain the range of motion gained through passive movement performed by the patient, completely unassisted. Resistive exercise is used to increase muscular strength, power, and endurance. It is performed against some external force, such as resistance by the therapist, by weights, or by an exercise machine. In general, the patient will move through passive, active assistive, active, to resistive exercise in stages.

In addition to dividing exercise into the four modes of delivery, there are three types of exercise. Isometric exercise is designed to strengthen muscle at the point in the range of motion where the force is applied. It is performed at zero speed with no joint or functional movement similar to tightening of muscles. It is used when the joint is immobilized to maintain tone and circulation. Isotonic exercise, also called Progressive Resistance Exercise (PRE) is dynamic and is performed against some form of resistance against the moving segment. Often this sort of isotonic exercise is performed on a piece of equipment or with weights. Isokinetic exercise is exercise performed on a device which provides a fixed speed with resistance throughout the range of motion.

> *Commentary*
>
> *The lack of any exercise program for months at a time in an insurance claim should make you ask a lot of questions. Rehabilitative exercise is a fundamental tenet of physical therapy. The basis of any rehab program is some type of exercise. If you have a patient on a rehab program and you are not exercising, even though your records are indicating a loss of motion-- then what is your rehab program doing? It's not addressing the problem.*
>
> *Nathaniel Randolph*

The objectives of exercise are to maintain or increase the range of motion, the muscle tone, the muscle strength, coordination, or endurance. A treatment program which does not include some form of exercise raises a question: it is possible that the therapist is simply allowing the patient to take palliative treatments without an rehabilitative or restorative goal in mind.

Electrical stimulation is provided by high voltage galvanic stimulators. It is used in the treatment of myofascial pain, in muscle spasm, and with edema associated with acute injury. It relieves pain, both acute and chronic pain. It is used to relieve muscle spasm, to increase the blood supply to a particular area, and it is used to decrease swelling or edema. It can be used in reeducation of muscles atrophied from disuse, and to prevent or retard muscle atrophy. Some units are said to build muscle size and strength. Electrical stimulation is not to be used in patients with heart disease or with a pacemaker. It should not be used across the upper thorax or the carotid sinus. It is contraindicated in cases of infection in the area of treatment, in cases of malignancy, pregnancy, vascular disease, or in patients with acute inflammation. In general, electrical stimulators should only be used by licensed professional therapists in accordance with a prescription from a physician.

Electrical stimulation is also used with motor or trigger points. Every nerve and muscle has a small area on the skin where it is most easily excited and where a visible contraction can be elicited with a minimal amount of electrical stimulation. The trigger point is usually locally tender. In the application of electrical stimulation, the electrical resistance of the skin itself is an important factor. Dry skin has a very high resistance to current, while wet skin has much lower resistance. Therefore it is recommended that electrical stimulation be preceded by some form of moist heat which will induce perspiration.

Massage is one of the oldest forms of treatment remedies. The purpose of massage is to produce therapeutic effect on tissues of the muscular and nervous systems of the body, and to stimulate local and general circulation. Massage produces mechanical stimulation or manipulation of the body tissues with rhythmically applied pressure and stretching. It is best performed with the hands. The physiological effects of massage are relaxation, sedation, and reduction of mental tension. The mechanical effects are to increase circulation. Massage is effective in stretching adhesions between muscle fibers and in mobilizing accumulations of fluid. Massage does not develop muscle strength and should not be used as a substitute for active exercise.

Massage relieves pain, mobilizes contracted tissues, and reduces swelling associated with trauma. It can be used to reduce spasm or increased sensitivity. It is contraindicated in cases of infection, malignancy, or skin disease; in cases of marked sensitivity where massage increases patient discomfort, it should be discontinued or temporarily postponed. Most massage treatments produce their effects as a result of a combination of physical, physiological, and psychological factors. Over the years, the basis for prescribing massage has evolved in a largely empirical manner, rather than as the result of any scientific research. Massage by itself does not restore function.[19]

Massage can take the form of stroking, compression, or percussion. Stroking can be varied from very light pressure through deep stroking, with variation in the rhythm, rate of movement and duration. Compression is a method of grasping and letting go of the tissues with one or both hands, in a lifting, rolling, or pressing movement. The purpose of compression is to loosen adhering tissues, and to speed up the flow of blood and lymph fluids. Percussion is a series of brief and rapid blows, in a hacking, clapping, or tapping motion, sometimes with added vibration or shaking movements. Percussion is rarely used in therapy, and is used in healthy individuals to aid in posture and to stimulate reflexes. Compression is sometimes used in the application of topical medications, as is deep stroking.[20]

TENS

Transcutaneous Electrical Nerve Stimulation or "TENS" is the application of low intensity, pulsed electrical current through the skin to a peripheral nerve or nerves to reduce pain. "TENS" involves placement of electrodes on the body over trigger points and the application of electrical impulses to the patient through the electrodes. Electrode placement is based on knowledge of neuroanatomy, and on previous experience. A "TENS Unit" is a battery-operated electrical impulse generator. The effectiveness of this treatment is documented for acute and chronic pain. The effectiveness of TENS is maximized by careful placement of the electrodes over the proper trigger point areas, and by the selection of proper stimulation variables: frequency, pulse width, intensity, and wave form. With variation of the current, the therapist can use a TENS treatment either to induce vasoconstriction, as with cold therapy, or vasodilation, as with heat treatment. But TENS is seldom a cure in either acute or chronic pain conditions. Rather, it is an effective way of reducing pain without medication so that other treatments like exercise can be performed. As with other modalities, the use of TENS strictly for palliative purposes, without combining it with a treatment plan aimed at rehabilitation, is an indication of poor usage in a clinical setting.

The effectiveness of TENS has been questioned in several recent studies, and care must be taken that it is not used as a primary clinical modality. In home use, therapists will rent or loan a unit to a patient for palliative use after evaluation and instruction. We must seriously question the use of TENS therapy by itself in an office setting. TENS is a palliative treatment of questionable effectiveness which is used primarily in an at-home setting -- not as a primary clinical modality. Payment for office use can be withheld without strong documentation regarding its effectiveness to justify the use of TENS in such a setting, showing that it is coupled with other treatments.

A PROFESSIONAL TREATMENT PROGRAM

The physical therapist has a wide variety of possible treatments or modalities to apply to achieve the goals of the treatment program with the patient. But it is not enough to say that the modality is one that is usually employed by therapists, or that it is more or less the sort of treatment one might expect with a particular condition. Rather, the treatment program should be appropriate to the individual patient, and should be based upon specific data gathered during the initial and follow- up examinations. As further information and data is gathered, and as progress is made, the treatment plan may be modified. But the overall purpose of the treatment should be explicit: there should be a set of goals to be achieved before discharge. In effect, the physical therapist should set a "discharge requirement" for the activity level of the individual patient and should work towards that level. Modalities which are part of the plan to work towards discharge are appropriate, those which simply take up time or which are palliative without connection to a treatment program are not appropriate.

All of these steps and procedures should be recorded, and if the claim comes into question, the therapist should be able to provide copies of the records. In Chapter Four, the correct methods of documenting the steps of evaluation and treatment are detailed.

The treatment techniques must be based on a rational planned program predicated on biomechanics, on physiology, on kinesiology, and on pathology. In designing the program, the data that is collected in the examination can be categorized and grouped to determine the modality of choice and the intensity of the application. For example, restricted motion can be categorized into "pain-inhibited" and "resistance-inhibited". If pain is the dominant limiting factor, the focus of the treatment plan should begin with pain reduction, protection of the injured part, a decrease of spasm, and a return to normal muscle tone. The sort of goals for treating musculoskeletal problems in the short term are protection of the injured area, decrease of activity level, and rest, decrease of pain, decrease of inflammation, decrease of intracapuslar effusion or synovitis, decrease of extracapsular edema or swelling, to increase the joint range of motion, and to educate and inform the patient. The long term goals may be to increase the musculotendinous flexibility, increase strength, power, endurance, to maintain cardiovascular endurance, to restore normal biomechanical function or to return to functional activity.

Thus professional treatment is more than the application of modalities which physical therapists have at their command. Rather, it is a set of procedures with specific short term and long term goals for the patient.

PROFESSIONALISM

The profession of physical therapy is one governed by changing state laws, and by changing technology. To the outsider, it may seem impossible to capture and define exactly what the limits of the profession are at a particular time and place and expect that picture to remain in force for several years. However, as insurance adjusters and claims review personnel examine the work of physical therapist professionals, they can keep several constants in mind.

By definition, a professional is one who performs his occupation to a high standard, and is not simply engaged in employment for the sake of income, as a technical employee. As a professional, a physical therapist should be able to make judgments as to appropriate treatment, duration and frequency of treatment, and should be able to recommend alteration or termination of a modality or a whole treatment program. Even in states without direct access, the therapist should be able to offer professional recommendations to the referring physician, if in the judgment of the therapist, a program should be altered or terminated. It is not enough to offer the "Nuremberg Defense," that is, the argument that "I was simply following orders."

In the area of physical therapy, the standard of professional performance holds the well-being of the patient as foremost. This means that the patient is provided with necessary, useful, and safe treatment, with the goal of restoring function. Some institutional arrangements can work against that professional goal, such as referral for profit. Yet direct access to the therapist can also lead to un-needed care, if the therapist is either careless or unscrupulous.

While it is not possible for a non-medical person to make independent judgments about the appropriateness of a particular treatment or modality, some picture of what is correct and incorrect may assist in identifying those practices which ought to be reviewed. The record should reflect an initial examination and some identification of subjective and objective symptoms. The therapist should indicate a plan of treatment, and there should be a sense of the goal of the plan. Therapy modalities should be logical for the plan, and should be altered or reviewed if little or no progress is achieved. Treatment should not be redundant, it should not last excessively long, and it should not be simply palliative.

The next chapter examines more closely some of the practices of physical therapy which represent types of over-utilization and poor utilization which the non-medical person can identify.

CHAPTER ONE ENDNOTES

1. ADTA Department of Practice: *Physical Therapy Practice, General Information*, (Alexandria, Virginia, no date, circa 1988), p. 2.
2. Ibid., p. 3-6.
3. Ibid., p. 26.
4. APTA
5. Ibid., "APTA Position Statement--Direct Access to Physical Therapy Services."
6. Ibid., Minnesota Chapter materials.
7. APTA, Department of Practice, *Referral for Profit* (Alexandria, Virginia, no date, circa April, 1990, page 3.
8. Ibid., page 32. Introduced as House Bill 444, section 54-278.3 of the Code of the Commonwealth of Virginia was amended in 1986 to reflect the concept of disclosure.
9. Ibid., p. 33-37.
10. J. B. Millard, "Conductive Heating," in Sidney Licht, *Therapeutic Heat and Cold* (2nd ed., Elizabeth Licht, Baltimore, 1972), p. 245.
11. Ibid., p. 246-247.
12. Bryan O. Scott, "Short Wave Diathermy," in Licht, p. 296.
13. Susan L. Michlovitz, *Thermal Agents in Rehabilitation* (Davis, Philadelphia, 1986), p. 151.
14. Fred Moor, "Microwave Diathermy, " in Licht, p. 316.
15. Ibid., p. 318.
16. Ibid, 319. Michlovitz, pp. 208-213.
17. Ibid., p. 160-161.
18. Justus Lehmann, "Ultrasound Therapy," in Licht, *Therapeutic Heat and Cold* pp. 360-361, 363.
19. Gertrude Beard and Elizabeth Wood, *Massage, Principles and Techniques*, (Saunders, Philadelphia, 1964), 36.
20. Ibid., p. 44-45.

2 Over-utilization

A Flaw in the System
The Importance of Utilization Review
"Proscriptive UR" and "Capitation"
Internal and External Utilization Review
Catagories of Wasteful Practices
Indications of Over-utilization
APTA Code of Ethics

OVER-UTILIZATION: A FLAW IN THE SYSTEM

In the last several decades, economic and legal factors, as well as the increasing use of physical therapy outside of the hospital setting, have stimulated "over-utilization" of physical therapy and other health care services. Under the American legal and insurance system, claims for bodily injuries, particularly in automobile insurance cases, frequently result in financial awards that are a multiple of the costs incurred. It is common for an insurance company to negotiate or for a court to award the victim of an accident direct reimbursement for lost wages, and to add to that amount three or more times the cost of medical and physical therapy expenses. Attorneys commonly base their contingency fees upon the amount recovered, usually totalling about 1/3 of the award or negotiated settlement.

When viewed in this light, it seems clear that forces which moderate pricing in free-market economies have broken down in the area of medical services. Under ordinary circumstances, the buyer and the seller of services have opposite interests, one to lower, and the other to raise the cost of the services. However, the monetary incentives for the parties involved in providing medical services in accident situations all point in the same direction. The claimant, the medical facilities providing the service, and the attorney all have an incentive to increase medical bills to the highest amount that could be regarded as reasonable and necessary.

To the extent that medical services are offered in a hospital setting, the hospital itself, as part of its accreditation agreement with the Joint Commission for Accreditation of Hospitals (JCAH), conducts internal "utilization review," or "UR" to ensure that medical and therapeutic practices are reasonable and necessary. In effect, hospitals have an internal self-policing system to protect against excessive utilization.

Over the 1970s and 1980s, as the number of practitioners offering health services outside of hospital settings increased, many decisions as to the provision of treatment were made simply by the patient and the provider, or by the patient and the attorney. Thus in those states which licensed physical therapists, chiropractors, and physicians to conduct rehabilitative therapy, many practitioners fell outside of the regular utilization review procedure of hospitals. In 1994, 42 states permitted physical therapists to conduct independent therapy businesses, that is, without a prescription or referral from a physician. Thus, they would work without the oversight of a referring physician, or a hospital-based utilization review committee.

Most states licensed physicians to conduct physical therapy, as well as independent physical therapists. Therefore, the term "physical therapy provider" encompasses both physicians and physical therapists, either in hospital or in independent clinics. In the cases of providers who operated outside of hospitals, internal or self utilization review was non-existent.

> *Commentary*
> *I have been an expert witness in numerous court cases involving excessive and unnecessary PT care. I have had the opportunity to review thousands of physical therapy claims from all areas of the country. These combined experiences have led me to, reluctantly, conclude that physical therapy has become one of the most over-utilized, misused and abused allied medical services in every area of practice, particularly in the treatment of soft tissue injuries. I have become alarmed, amazed and appalled and sometimes embarrassed by the abusive practices of many members of our profession....*
>
> *Nathaniel Randolph*
> *PT Bulletin, May 17, 1989*

Whether injured patients seek health care from licensed, privately-practicing physical therapists, or from physicians offering physical therapy in their own offices, every economic incentive points in the direction of increasing the utilization of physical therapy to, and in many cases, beyond what is necessary and reasonable. Although patients might find it onerous to attend physical therapy sessions long after the benefit from the therapy has ceased, if they keep in mind that for every fifty-dollar session with the therapist their fraction of the final triple damage award will amount to about fifty dollars, they have a direct economic motive to continue to attend. In effect, triple damages have the effect of 1) paying for the unneeded therapy, 2) paying for the services of the attorney, and 3) paying the patient to receive the unneeded therapy.

Current practices in the provision of private medical services, therefore, have outgrown the capacity of the free marketplace to regulate costs. In this marketplace, powerful incentives to increase prices operate unopposed by incentives to reduce them. The market, as currently constituted, actually encourages abuse. All over the nation, the urban areas represent a disproportionate amount of the abuse and cost in these areas. Several factors work together to increase costs in the cities: their concentrations of therapists, medical facilities, heavy traffic patterns, large numbers of "fender-bender" accidents, and concentrations of attorneys and physicians specializing in bodily injury claims. A whole "micro-economy" will develop out of a single automobile fender-bender accident. In a large city such as Washington, D.C., the number of physical therapists listed in the yellow pages in 1975 would occupy two or three column-inches; by 1994, the listings occupied several pages.

As long as insurance companies could pass the cost of increasing claims through to the purchaser of the insurance in the form of increased premiums, even the insurance companies had no incentive to hold down the cost of treatment. But greed drove the system. As medical costs climbed and insurance premiums climbed along with them, a growing public outcry against both resulted in increasing distress at the failure of the market place in this area.

When the provision of health care, especially wasteful health care in bodily injury cases funded by auto insurance became a public and a social issue, a motive for control of the system came in. By public referendum, the State of California enacted a bill putting a ceiling on insurance premiums. This was only one indication of the public rebellion at the escalation of the costs. As a consequence, insurance companies have been under pressure to identify and control excessive expenses, which before, slipped through the controls of the market place and ran wild. While legitimate use of physical therapy soared over the years, over-utilization also soared.

Still another economic factor contributing to over utilization of physical therapy is the proliferation of therapy equipment manufacturers and new types of expensive devices and systems. For example, a recent issue of one of the professional journals of the PT community, carried full page advertisements for hot pack heaters, an iontophoretic drug delivery system for tendinitis, six separate computer software systems to improve reporting, two different mobilization tables for use in rehabilitation, a weight-training machine, and a TENS system. This list does not reflect half-page advertisements, nor other items, including small swimming pools, electronic devices, diathermy, thermography, and massage equipment, that are constantly promoted and sold. Therapists purchasing the equipment, particularly that which is therapeutic or diagnostic in nature, have every incentive to use it as often as possible and to bill for the service in order to make the investment worthwhile.

Salesmen who sell the equipment make the point that the machine will make the therapist money. A certain level of usage of the machine will pay it off; further use of the new "modality" will represent income for the therapist. Thus the advertising, the funds invested, and the sales pitch all point in the direction of increasing usage and increasing billing. A therapist who has purchased equipment will be under an incentive to use it as much as possible; there will be a motive to use the equipment even when it is not necessary for the patient.

> *Commentary*
>
> *Many medical practice consultants and physical therapy equipment dealers are directing their marketing strategies towards physicians to provide physical therapy in order to increase their profits. This has resulted in an incredible amount of over- utilization of physical therapy services. Many of the clinics billing for physical therapy are poorly equipped, containing only a hot pack unit and maybe an ultrasound or electrical stimulator. On the other hand, there are some large, well-managed clinics that gross millions per year.*
>
> *Nathaniel Randolph*
PT Bulletin, May 17, 1989.

Since many doctors now practice "Defensive Medicine," that is, providing treatment and care that might be unnecessary, in order to avoid malpractice suits, many patients will find themselves subject to a wide range of tests and may receive duplicative treatment. This factor has also contributed to climbing health care costs. Attorneys point out that the American people expect excellent health care, and if they do not get it, they might sue.[1]

There are several organizations with contrary incentives, that is, with definite financial motivations to hold down excessive medical claims costs generated through fraud, abuse, and over-utilization of care. However, their effectiveness is blunted because their participation occurs after medical services have been provided. In addition to casualty insurance companies which might be able to decrease their losses in the bodily-injury coverage area, self-insurers, workmen's compensation insurance firms, and state-owned workmen's compensation funds are beginning to seek outside review of their medical claims. Some physicians and other health care professionals who previously conducted internal utilization review in the hospital setting, are now finding it possible to serve as consultants in outside review cases.[2] In the area of private firms which provide their own health care to employees, corporations such as Northwestern Bell, Control Data Corporation, and Honeywell, Incorporated, are seeking internal or outside review to lower costs. In its simplest form, a review could analyze the costs and practices of various providers, and exclude the most excessive or the most expensive. In effect, that system represents an employer shopping for the best service. In more complex approaches, a case-by-case utilization review can also serve to lower expenses.[3]

Some types of injuries result in objective medical conditions which are easily diagnosed and measured. For example, when a wound or a broken bone heals, the healing can be detected and can be objectively documented. However, strains and sprains, and other "soft-tissue injuries" to the musculoskeletal system, often result in conditions which can be evaluated only subjectively. Such injuries are very difficult to identify and measure objectively. For example, one patient might complain of pain, while another would find a similar degree of pain or discomfort merely inconvenient. Thus, the determination of what conditions related to soft-tissue injuries continue to need treatment is a very subjective one. Although there exist a number of means of objectifying and measuring soft-tissue diagnoses, this particular type of injury tends to generate the majority of disputed claims over the appropriate level of treatment.

The discrepancy between subjective and objective assessments creates ample room for debate over what constitutes reasonable and necessary care. In our system, the judgement of such disputes can ultimately come before a court of law. A claimant with no real impairment might malinger, or "fake" a condition. Or, a genuine condition, for which there is genuine treatment, can be exaggerated and the therapy prolonged, with the claimant and the therapist both motivated to increase the expense to the greatest extent possible. Both of these scenarios constitute fraud. For these reasons, soft-tissue injuries tend to be the ones that most often result in litigation. In an automobile accident, often the patient and the physisian or therapist will see the accident as an opportunity to make money.

When someone is injured at home, say stretching neck muscles while painting, the sole object of health care is to fix the sore neck as quickly as possible. However, if a personal-injury, liability accident is involved, other forces besides health care needs begin to operate. Accidents produce claims. Claims against another party are valued by the amount and cost of the medical care and the lost time at work. When patients become claimants, because of the economics involved, more care is given. Many personal injury attorneys become the de facto directors of the health care, and they press for more care. Thus, an extraordinary amount of care becomes directed, not by medical needs, but by claim needs.

> *Commentary*
>
> *If you take your run of the mill, average, minor, soft-tissue injury, your fender-bender accident, with minimal to moderate damage, where you have no injury, no broken bones, just a back or neck sprain or strain, soft-tissue, musculoskeletal strain, and you look at the claims at what is being paid out, how many reviewers have seen the defendant making those claims? It is <u>always</u> the claimant. Yet, the simple laws of physics would say both parties would receive the same amount of injury. But only the one who sues gets the massive claims, whereas those who run the red light--those guys never got hurt. Oftentimes, you will get someone who initially makes a claim for injury; then several days down the road, the police will charge him with a traffic violation or indicate that the other party was not at fault, and suddenly the patient will stop treatment. One of the best cures is that the patient finds that he does not have a court case.*
>
> *Nathaniel Randolph*

In many cases, outright fraud has been identified in the padding of bills and in schemes to artificially inflate medical costs. One evaluation in 1989 placed the extent of fraudulent medical claims in the United States at $16 billion annually. Moves by the federal Health Care Facilities Administration (HCFA) and by the Department of Health and Human Services to investigate and monitor health care have focussed on fraud. In New Jersey, insurance companies themselves were investigated, due to the fact that under the state law, many fraudulent claims were referred to a state fund without investigation or utilization review.[4]

IMPORTANCE OF UTILIZATION REVIEW

With health care practitioners operating in a free- enterprise system, licensed to provide services but largely unregulated beyond the state licensing bureau, it is a simple matter for claimants with soft-tissue injuries to increase levels of therapy and treatment. In this setting, it is crucial that some form of utilization review be established to help control escalating claims, and to control the consequently escalating insurance premiums to cover the cost of the inflated claims. If the utilization review is logical, objective, and clearly understandable by the lay person, it will provide a useful tool in determining if and when over-utilization abuses have occurred, and where reimbursement should be allowed for necessary and reasonable care.

Clarifying these technical issues for benefit of the lay person is important because individuals outside the health care professions are often called upon to help resolve disputes. The lay people involved include not only juries in some court cases, but claims adjusters, claims reviewers, attorneys, and judges.

A great many methods have been adopted by utilization reviewers to examine the services of physical therapists, in independent and institutional settings. The identification of evidence of over-utilization is often a matter of simple logic, of identifying inconsistencies, and spotting exaggerated or excessive claims of treatment. The first line of defense against excessive claims in the soft tissue area is, of course, the claims adjuster at the insurance company. However, insurance companies commonly allocate only $2 to $5 in time spent in processing the average claim, which means that the adjuster can spend only a few minutes reviewing each packet of documents. From this brief look at the documentation, the adjuster must spot difficulties for further internal review, for outside review, or for further investigation.

In the most obvious cases, an insurance adjuster might call for an Independent Medical Examination (IME) of the patient to determine whether the condition and treatment seemed more than adequate, necessary, or reasonable. However, since in the typical case, the excessive treatment only comes to the attention of the insurance company after the services have been billed, then the billing itself, and the surrounding documentation will be closely scrutinized to determine whether there has been excessive treatment, or whether the claim should be honored as a legitimate, necessary, and reasonable expense.

Documentation can reveal to the auditor, utilization reviewer, consultant, attorney, or claims adjuster, a series of irregularities which raise a flag indicating that a bill has been padded. However, human ingenuity in such matters has led to a wide range of possible, less easily detectable ways to run up a bill. Clearly, the simplest way to maximize the payment is to increase the duration or frequency of visits to therapy. For certain types of injuries, a pattern of increased duration or frequency will leap out, statistically, and might be detected on the basis of numbers alone.

Statistics thus allow one to take a "computer audit" of claims. Under a variety of these systems, claims review firms can examine an insurer's files and identify those particular claims which reflect excessive amounts of billing, extensive duration, or extensive frequency. In each case, those claims with numbers which represent wide variations from the median amount, duration, or frequency for a particular diagnosis can be identified from the statistics alone, and can be pulled for more intensive investigation. A certain diagnosis has a usual number of treatments, and a certain level of billing.

Of course, such identification of a problem case does not necessarily provide enough information to deny a claim, particularly when it is kept in mind that the denial might be tested in court. Statistical irregularities might be considered indicators of a problem, but they do not alone constitute proof of abuse. Indeed, in any range of expenses, one might logically expect to see numbers at both extremes on a graph of costs, and the mere existence of a pattern of high bills or extensive treatment is no proof of abuse.

In this connection, the federal agency concerned with setting standards for payment in Medicare cases, the Health Care Facilities Administration (HCFA), in 1989 established layers of statistical filters or "screens" to sift through their case load and identify possible instances of unnecessary care. In effect the HCFA screens establish numbers of weeks, and numbers of treatments which are statistically expected for a great many conditions and rehabilitative situations. Cases which exceed the norms are flagged for further review. Yet HCFA warns its own personnel, health-care providers, and insurance "intermediaries" not to reject claims on the basis of exceeding the screen limitation alone. Simply defining an "average" duration or frequency of treatments, HCFA points out, does not justify the denial of all claims at the high end of the range. It simply identifies the likeliest cases for the most profitable expenditure of review energies.

Although the screens established by HCFA are specific to Medicare claims, federal limits on fees can serve as guidelines for treatment in automobile cases and workmen's compensation cases. Pennsylvania has adopted a system of using the Medicare allowable payment schedule or "fee schedule" as guidelines for auto insurance cases, and other states are considering their incorporation in both auto and workmen's compensation insurance legislation.[5]

Beyond billing for excessively long or frequent treatments, there are many other practices which would indicate treatment that was excessive, unnecessary or unreasonable. High (and therefore unreasonable) rates might be charged for necessary treatments. Unnecessary treatments for a condition might have been applied. Treatments which are redundant might have been used. Several different kinds or duplicative modalities of treatment might have been used in a situation usually requiring only one. The same treatment might have been billed several times. There might be billings for treatments never given or received.

Among the practices which are more difficult for the initial claims reviewer to identify are "unbundling" and "stacking" of treatments or modalities. Unbundling might be defined as the practice of claiming that a single treatment with several aspects was in fact a number of separate treatments; in effect, the package of treatments, given at the same time with the same equipment, was "unbundled" or taken apart in order for the therapist to claim a charge for each element. An example might be the application of a heat treatment to three areas of the back. The hot packs would be taken by the therapist from a machine, and applied, within seconds of each other, to three different areas of the body: shoulder, upper and lower back. Yet the bill might show three separate treatments, "hot pack to thoracic area," "hot pack to lumbar area," and "hot pack to shoulder." It would not be unusual for such unbundling to escape the reviewer on a quick read of the file. Only a minimal amount of additional time is required to make up the additional two hot packs. A treatment which should cost about $60 would thus end up being billed at the rate of $180.

Modality stacking represents several redundant treatments applied to the same area in the same session, again unnecessarily. Two forms of superficial or deep heat, ultrasound diathermy and hotpacks might both be applied to the same area, where one modality would have achieved the same effect. The treatments are thus "stacked" one upon the other without any therapeutic advantage to the patient.

While the adjuster or claims reviewer might not be sure whether multiple modalities had taken place from looking at the file, cases which appear to include either bundling or stacking should be submitted for more senior review and possibly for peer review.

"PROSPECTIVE UR" AND "CAPITATION"

Prospective utilization review and the capitation payment method can be seen as two different strategies used by employers and insurance companies to improve cost control in health care benefits. Prospective utilization review means a system of prior review or pre-authorization for health care, with a review of the need for the services before hospitalization, and even before surgery. The problem with prospective, rather than the more common retrospective utilization review, is that employers run risks for liability from the delay or from rejected cases.

In 1990, the American Medical Association house of delegates disapproved of hospital preadmission review used by some commercial insurers and managed care firms. Medicare review in Georgia and Blue Cross/Blue Shield review in Minnesota were particularly singled out for AMA criticism. In Georgia, a utilization review firm had recommended denial of a large number of outpatient claims. In Minnesota, the Blue Cross system targeted cases for review based upon a set of standards derived from an expert consensus panel. Both practices, the AMA claimed, tended to set falsely objective standards and to substitute them for physician judgments.

Some Health Maintenance Organizations (HMOs), have implemented "capitation" standards for medical costs. Under a system of capitation, a set monthly payment for each individual for a package of health care services is established as a ceiling. The advantages of capitation are that it places a ceiling on the employers' cost, and reduces the incentive to provide unnecessary treatments. On the other hand, capitation does not discourage unnecessary treatments, as long as they fall within the prescribed ceilings, and could even encourage the over-utilization of services within the range. For example, if the capitation rate allowed six weeks of therapy for rehabilitation of a particular disability, but the provider found progress tapering off after two weeks, that provider might be tempted to continue to the allowed ceiling. Furthermore, the system could encourage practitioners to raise their fees to match the allowable ceiling. Under capitation, the therapist is at risk if the services are utilized more than predicted, either illegitimately, or legitimately. From the viewpoint of the health care providers, retrospective utilization, although subjecting the provider's records to close scrutiny by outsiders, provides a fairer means of limiting health care costs than either prospective review or capitation.[7]

INTERNAL AND EXTERNAL UTILIZATION REVIEW

In a hospital, utilization review is conducted by health care professionals, in a structured setting in which employees, answerable to supervisors, must justify their actions or face possible internal discipline. In the open marketplace of health care provision by independent practitioners, no such structured disciplinary system is present. Outside utilization review thus finds a place. In fact, the service is rapidly becoming an industry in itself, with a number of firms devoted to utilization review selling their services to insurance companies and to large firms involved in self-insuring their employees.[8]

Nevertheless, we find that even in hospitals, the rate of unnecessary medical care provided to automobile victims greatly exceeds that for other patients. In the hospital setting, with its internal utilization review, economic and administrative incentives to give excessive care can readily generate gray-area abuses. In 1990, it was estimated that as much as fifty percent of the medical care given in automobile accident cases was unnecessary and wasteful. One estimate put the total dollar amount paid out in fraudulent or abusive auto insurance medical claims at $16 billion annually. Much of this unneeded care was provided in hospitals having internal systems of utilization review. In many hospitals, physical therapy, along with some other auxiliary departments, such as the x-ray laboratory, is one of the profitable services. Hospital administrators, faced with their own sets of financial pressures, cannot afford to ignore the profitability of over-utilization of physical therapy. They are often more lenient in decisions, allowing longer stays and longer treatments for casualty patients to make up for the loss of revenue in other areas (such as Medicare) where a stricter level of utilization review is required. Medicare or Medicaid simply would not pay for excessive hospitalization, whereas the casualty insurance company involved in a bodily injury case might be more likely to accept the billing and make the payment.

Even though automobile insurance providers are beginning to apply guidelines like those of HCFA to non-federally funded health care and conducting more thorough utilization review, excessive and unnecessary claims continue to appear. Recognizing that the courts have upheld some very extensive claims in bodily injury liability cases, hospitals and all therapy providers are justified in believing that automobile insurance is more likely to offer coverage of gray-area therapy than is Medicare, with its stricter and required standards of review. Since the ultimate resolution of auto liability cases is the tort court, rather than the Medicare UR forum, the hospitals and outside health care providers are well aware that a less stringent standard, subject to lay interpretation and to a natural sympathy for the victim on the part of both judges and juries, is at work.

As UR spreads as a practice operated by independent consulting firms, it moves into the vacuum created in the market system to provide a tool by which insurers can hold down the escalating costs of medical claims. Medical claims review firms moved, in 1990, towards setting up their own accreditation service, in order to establish a professional approach. The Utilization Review Accreditation Commission (URAC) is a coalition of UR firms establishing voluntary standards of utilization review.[9] The firms in this coalition are also members of the American Managed Care Review Association (AMCRA).

Although some individual doctors have resisted medical claims utilization review systems as intrusive or harassing, the American Medical Association has responded to the growth of outside utilization review firms with the view that external utilization review can be a valuable tool to control medical costs. The review firms have sought the cooperation of the AMA in developing responsible and professional approaches.[10]

It is difficult to separate the different types of over-utilization into ethical categories, because each particular case will reflect a different situation. Logically, however, one might say that there are three broad categories of over-utilization, from the ethical point of view. They are Waste, Abuse, and Fraud. Waste would represent those cases in which a wasteful treatment was provided, with no particular benefit to the patient. Abuse of the system might come in those cases in which either the patient, or the therapist, or the doctor, set the treatment level intentionally high or engaged in redundant treatment in order to escalate the medical bills. A variety of means of reporting modalities so as to increase the revenue from relatively inexpensive or brief treatments is also abusive. Fraud would come in cases of claiming treatment that did not take place, in claiming a condition which did not exist, or in collusive extension of treatment well after the condition had been corrected or maximum improvement had been achieved.

Although some practices in the over-utilization area can be regarded as fraudulent, others fall in a gray area, and represent only an abuse, a stretching of ethical principles. But it is clear that the economic incentives are there for the claimant, for the attorney, and for the health care practitioner to push the limit of reasonableness and necessity in care. In many cases, the claims for soft tissue injuries will lead to only a few hundred dollars for medical treatment, but several thousand dollars worth of palliative physical therapy.

Thus cases of over-utilization run the gamut from outright fraud, through unethical overuse, through wasteful or redundant treatment, through simple error and poor planning. From the perspective of the insurer, all over-utilization of treatment, regardless of the motivation or the degree of ethical lapse, should be denied. Those cases in which there is more ethical misbehavior on the part of the health-care provider and the patient will be easier for the insurance company to win in court; however, all over-utilization, even when innocent of fraud or abuse, will be subject to identification and claims denial by the reviewer.

CATEGORIES OF WASTEFUL PRACTICES

The definition of necessary medical care should be kept in mind. Necessary care is directed toward getting the patient better and out of treatment as quickly as possible. Unnecessary care does not contribute towards these goals. In general, when patients are involved in accidents in which there is insurance coverage, they receive longer periods of care, more care, and a wide range of wasteful care. Much of the over use of physical therapy is a matter of poor practice or waste, rather than unethical or illegal behavior. Several types of over-utilization reflecting unneeded and wasteful care can result in claims which are denied. Denials for poor utilization have stood up in court, when litigated. Even though a judge or jury might find it easier to deny a claim when unethical practices can be identified, the courts have also sustained denials on grounds of waste. In general, unnecessary and wasteful care, as distinct from cases of ethical abuse or outright, intentional fraud, can be traced to four types of causes. They are:

1.) lack of organized approach to a defined treatment goal
    -unnecessary care
    -palliative care
    -excessive frequency
    -excessive duration
2.) excessive charges
3.) misapplication or misemployment of technology
4.) outdated and unproven technology applications.

Lack of an organized approach and a defined treatment goal can result from several causes, which can be identified when closely examining a case. Indications or evidence of lack of planning include an incomplete or careless history or record of examination, the lack of explicit treatment plans, a failure to note the patient's responses, and a poorly documented statement of the patient's progress under the care. Furthermore, we sometimes find that there is no modification of a plan to meet changing needs on the part of the patient. Sometimes a pattern of random office visits and consultations will reveal a lack of plan. Another flag indicating a poor plan of care would be aborted hospital visits, where a patient checked in and was then dismissed because the visit had no function or was unnecessary. One would normally expect a record to show decreasingly frequent office visits as the patient made progress. But if a patient was not progressing, then a change in treatment plan should be shown. Sometimes neither occurs.

Often treatment is provided to unrelated musculoskeletal problems, for example, a pre-existing condition. The record might reveal that a patient had been visiting the provider for treatment of an existing lower back pain. As a result of an accident, the condition might legitimately have been aggravated. Thus, some treatment to restore the patient to the status as of the date of the accident, under the bodily injury claim would be legitimate. But treatment beyond that point would be a case of insurance abuse. In such situations, the judgment call would be quite difficult; the guideline, however, is that the insurance should cover restoring the patient to the status as it was prior to the accident. Continued palliative treatment or continued restorative treatment beyond that point is not the auto-insurance carrier's responsibility.

Excessive charges can easily be billed in many bodily injury cases, where the patient is hospitalized. In effect, the patient is in a monopoly situation, where the health care provider is in charge of decisions and pricing. The provider or hospital may take the attitude that it is an easy reimbursement, and find little incentive to control costs. Quite the contrary. The incentive is to maximize the care. The review of reasonableness and necessity may be neglected. The hospital is under an incentive to shift overhead costs from those less able to pay to those from whom it appears easier to collect.

Another kind of non-fraudulent over-utilization is the misapplication of technology. For example, we sometimes see duplicate sets of x-rays performed within two or three days of each other. Often one set is taken in the emergency room, and then the physician provider will order another one on the first office visit, and often a third set will be taken by a consulting specialist. The x-rays are available to the health care provider from the hospital and the second or third set is therefore unnecessary. A casual review of part of the file would not reveal that the technology had been misused, since one would not be aware of the first set of x-rays at the hospital if only the records of a later provider were reviewed. Thus it is important to review all the care received in a case, and not just the care of one provider. Frequently physicians will insist on taking a fresh set of x-rays even when aware of previous ones, on the grounds that their equipment gives better resolution, or that there will be a delay in obtaining the prior x-rays. Such justifications for duplication show how difficult it is to judge whether or not the over-utilization was intentional simply to increase the fee base, or whether it derived from a more legitimate motivation, and was wasteful through honest oversight or concern for speed and reliability.

With so much of the testing, especially laboratory tests, now easily performed in the physician's office, there arises another type of overuse of technology: testing for an ailment or condition unrelated to the accident. Physicians who buy expensive machines are quite likely to run tests on each patient when reimbursement is expected from an automobile insurance carrier. Nearly 900 different types of tests can be run on blood alone; yet rarely do accident claims need most of those tests. Machines to test and measure range of motion, for example, are not necessary, as the physicians and physical therapists have training in the skill of measuring range of motion without specialized equipment.

The definition of a necessary test is very simple. When a test is likely to provide new or additional information which will affect the treatment of the patient, it can be regarded as necessary. Thus if one test, like a CT scan has shown a bulging disc, a second test, such as an MRI can sometimes be unnerving. Blood tests of liver or kidney functions when an individual has a sore neck are clearly not medically necessary for the injury in question, yet such blood tests will show up in accident case after accident case, and insurance companies will often pay such claims without question.

A common misuse of technology occurs with the use of equipment whose sole purpose is palliative, but which does not aim at restoration of function. While treatment for pain in connection with therapy is legitimate, continued treatment whose only function is the temporary relief of pain represents over- utilization.

Another very common misuse of technology occurs with Transcutaneous Electrical Nerve Stimulation [TENS] units. A TENS unit is a battery operated electrical impulse generator with electrodes applied to trigger points, that is, the most sensitive point on a muscle, also known as a "nerve motor point." TENS units have a legitimate use in controlling pain; however, they are commonly misused or overused in patients with minor soft- tissue injuries. Providers frequently order TENS applications on the initial office visit without first establishing the requirements for the use of one. A typical charge for the purchase of a TENS unit for home use might be $500 to $700. Often times a patient is brought into the treatment center for one application of the TENS unit, when in fact that particular unit is designed for home-use and self-use. It could have been used by the patient himself, either on a rental or sale basis. The purchase of the machine, whether used or not, represents a quick inflation of the bill, and occasionally an attorney will order such a machine sent to the patient, simply to inflate the total bill.

In the area of suspect or worthless technology, we find obsolete tests being used as diagnostic tools, or obsolete equipment being used to treat patients. The accuracy of diagnoses and the effectiveness of care based on the use of obsolete equipment are highly questionable. Such equipment cannot be properly calibrated and there are no current technician training programs. On the other extreme, we find many new machines and technologies which have not yet been approved by the FDA, and therefore the devices have not been proven to be of value. Some that have been tested have been shown to be valueless. In such cases, insurance companies are being asked to pay huge sums merely to have someone turn a useless machine on and off. The patient does not benefit, and in fact, the patient may actually be in danger from such equipment.

Some claims are filed with the justification that a practice or a fee is "usual and customary" in the profession. State laws and court practice require that insurers pay what is "reasonable and necessary." Sometimes, the two principles of what is acceptable or appropriate come into conflict. If some of the practices just described are usual and customary in some of the areas of practice, they might appear to be justified, even though they are not "reasonable or necessary." For example, if it is customary for every physician in a state to order x-rays of a patient entering the office, regardless of whether there were prior x-rays, and if it were usual for each physical therapist to apply an isokinetic test to the patient, those procedures, although usual and customary, would not meet the reasonable and necessary guideline.

The difference is between what is correct, versus what is done. The problem or flaw is that if one uses as review parameters the usual and customary rule, the parameters are being set by the same community that the system is intended to control. The same principle applies to fee levels. Even though a fee is usual or customary does not necessarily justify its basis. If practitioners are regularly marking up the cost of their treatments by 500 per cent, we have an objective measure that the fees, although usual and customary, have become excessive.

INDICATIONS OF OVER-UTILIZATION

In the claims review process, certain indications of over- utilization are strikingly obvious, and suggest more direct abuse. The presence of any of these indicators should alert a claims adjuster or claims reviewer that there is a serious problem:

1. NO INITIAL TREATMENT OR TREATMENT DELAY. If there was no treatment until more than a week after the accident, the record would suggest the possibility that the treatment derived from an attempt to build a bill, and should be looked at closely.
2. GAP IN TREATMENT. Any cases in which there is an unexplained gap or lapse of more than two weeks in treatment should be scrutinized.
3. BIOFEEDBACK CARE. Any cases in which biofeedback was ordered or billed should be closely scrutinized. That technology remains unproven as therapy, although some practitioners use it for diagnostic purposes.
4. THERMOGRAPHY testing, which although expensive, has no proven reliability in determining injury, and also bears investigation. The machine measures the heat areas on the surface of the skin; theoretically it would indicate the area of the body with pain. However, a hot spot can be caused by any number of factors, not necessarily blood-flow to an injured or painful spot. The test might be $300 or $400, but show absolutely nothing except that the patient had a warm area. It is another category of technology-use which many insurance companies now automatically reject. Courts have ruled both ways on whether or not to accept charges for thermography, although insurance companies are contesting its legitimacy, and the thermogram defenders are fighting a loosing battle.[11]
5. MULTIPLE PROVIDERS OR "PINGPONGING." Cases involving multiple providers to evaluate the same problem are indications of an attempt to run up a bill.
6. EXCESSIVELY LONG OR EXCESSIVELY FREQUENT CARE. Bodily injury cases in which soft-tissue treatment extends beyond six or eight weeks for minor soft-tissue injuries, are another category of probable abuse.

Any cases with these obvious indications of over-utilization should be subjected to close utilization review to determine whether abuse has occurred. If effective, a utilization review system will identify inappropriate care. Furthermore it will protect patients in that it will require proper treatment planning and prevent random unnecessary testing, unneeded hospitalization, and ineffective treatment. A solid review system will require that all bills are justified, and will ensure that all justified bills are reimbursed.

Many of the evidences of abuse are strikingly obvious. In outpatient physical therapy settings, it is ordinary and accepted practice (one taught in the physical therapy schools) to offer therapy for soft tissue injury on the basis of about three office visits a week. If the records of a case reveal daily visits, particularly more than one week after the first treatment, that would be a possible indication of over-use. In one recent case, Mrs. Adams missed a couple of those daily visits, and the record showed that the therapist did not call Mrs. Adams, but called her attorney. That told the claims reviewer something.

Pingponging is also one of the most obvious evidences of abuse. Often a record will show a visit on one day to a family doctor, the next day to an orthopedist, the next to a neurologist, the next day back to the doctor or even another specialist such as a dentist for the work associated with neck injuries. Substantial costs are created, and physical therapy itself has not even begun. With that pingponging effect, it does not take long for the bills to escalate into the thousands of dollars. A close look at the records in pingponged cases may reveal that the doctor reports a neck, back and shoulder injury, while a second doctor will record only a problem with the back. Then the therapist, we will find, delivered therapy to only one of the areas. Thus, the attempt to inflate a bill through multiple referrals can backfire on the claimant, when there are discrepancies in diagnoses or in the record from one treatment- provider to another. Discrepancies of all sorts in the documentation are crucial to identifying over- utilization; they are more likely to show up in fraudulent or abusive claims where the patient was pingponged. Too many cooks spoil the broth.

In one case, a Mr. Brown was released from the emergency room after an accident with a report that said there was nothing wrong, and that he had no complaints. The record showed that three days later, Mr. Brown sought therapy, and over the next two months, he accrued four thousand dollars worth of bills from two doctors. Now, it is entirely possible that Mr. Brown fell down the steps and developed an injury after his release from the hospital emergency room, and really needed the treatments he received. But if the emergency room diagnosis which followed the accident showed no problem, and he was released without complaint, and he had another accident two days later, or on the way out of the hospital, the claim was being filed on the wrong insurance policy. In Mr. Brown's case, the claim seemed suspicious, and on review, it was rejected.

Injuries requiring several months of expensive treatment most likely should have some symptomology present on the day of the injury. A patient may not go immediately to a doctor, but then may turn up three weeks later, with an attorney. However, sometimes a patient shows up, legitimately, with a nagging pain, which did in fact come from an accident. But when they go to their attorney first, it makes you wonder.

Still another indication of misuse of services comes with a few Registered Physical

Therapists (RPTs) "selling" their signatures. One therapist made it a practice to commute from out of state to review the case files of a doctor who claimed to employ licensed personnel conducting therapy. In fact, a Licensed Practical Nurse delivered therapy. The RPT would fly in every few weeks, review her backlog of files, and co-sign the day to day notes. He was not simply approving what she had done, he was fraudulently claiming that he had seen the patient on a daily basis, even though his visits were occasional. His license has subsequently been challenged in both his home state and in the state where the therapy was delivered. The office manager of the clinic put in writing the schedule and practice, clearly documenting the abuse.

In some areas there is such a shortage of physical therapists, it is often common for doctors to have a therapist come in and review their notes, and evaluate the patients, and the assistants will provide the treatment. Each state has different laws pertaining to how many treatments can be administered without supervision. In the state of Maryland, ten treatments can be administered without a licensed therapist checking the work; in the state of Virginia, five treatments. Despite the variation from state to state, the intent of the law is to ensure that the assistants do not work unsupervised; rather the concept of utilizing assistants was to help in the provision of home care. Under this system, the assistants would visit the patient at home, and the therapist would check once a week or so to assess the patient's progress. But in no state was the law intended to have an outside therapist come into an office and sign off on the progress notes prepared by unsupervised assistants.

Commentary

While physical therapy is well-defined in most state practice acts, one thing that needs to be better defined is who can practice physical therapy. In most states physical therapy regulations require that physical therapy be performed by a physical therapist and that aides and assistants be supervised by the physical therapist....

The most serious form of unethical practice that I have seen is physical therapists selling their signatures to "legitimize" PT treatment provided by unlicensed personnel working in physician-owned physical therapy clinics. This fraudulent practice is, for lack of a better word, disgusting.

Nathaniel Randolph
PT Bulletin, May 17, 1989

APTA CODE OF ETHICS

The American Physical Therapy Association [APTA] has established a Code of Ethics, a statement regarding Standards of Care, and a Guide for Professional Conduct which speak to the question of over-utilization of physical therapy services. The Preamble of the Code of Ethics of the APTA is provided below.

The Code of Ethics sets forth ethical principles for the physical therapy profession. Members of this profession are responsible for maintaining and promoting ethical practice. This Code of Ethics, adopted by the American Physical Therapy Association, shall be binding on physical therapists who are members of the Association.

Principle 1
Physical therapists respect the rights and dignity of all individuals.
Principle 2
Physical therapists comply with the laws and regulations governing the practice of physical therapy.
Principle 3
Physical therapists accept responsibility for the exercise of sound judgment.
Principle 4
Physical therapists maintain and promote high standards in the provision of physical therapy services.
Principle 5
Physical therapists seek remuneration for their services that is deserved and reasonable.
Principle 6
Physical therapists provide accurate information to the consumer about the profession and about those services they provide.
Principle 7
Physical therapists accept the responsibility to protect the public and the profession from unethical, incompetent, or illegal acts.
Principle 8
Physical therapists participate in efforts to address the health needs of the public.
Adopted by the House of Delegates, June, 1981, Amended June, 1987

Under the APTA Code of Ethics, Principal 3 recognizes that physical therapists must accept responsibility for sound judgment, and the unequivocal ultimate reason for providing services must be the individual patient's need for the service. Principal 5 states that personal financial reward must be reasonable and deserved.

In particular, the supplementary Standards of Care of the APTA states in Standard 13, <u>Reevaluation</u>: "The physical therapist reevaluates the individual and modifies the plan of care as indicated." The Guide for Conduct, which spells out the implications of the Code, states in provision 3.3.C: "Over- utilization caused by continuing physical therapy services beyond the point of possible benefit or by providing services more frequently than necessary for maximum therapeutic effect, is unethical." Therefore, according to the APTA, services should be ended or re-directed when it is clear that services will not change the outcome or the patient's status. The Guide to Practice is explicitly clear that treatment should be delivered as infrequently as will produce the greatest gain for the individual receiving the services.[12]

The APTA's Judicial Committee restates and publishes these basic ethical imperatives. The Committee spelled out some possible problems in a position paper in the APTA Journal. Tracing a hypothetical case, the Judicial Committee indicated that a therapist should continue to give therapy only as long as the patient was showing improvement towards maximum potential. If it becomes clear that the patient will never reach the goals, "even with additional time and treatment...the therapist is required to inform" the patient of that judgement and to discontinue treatment. "In any event," the committee pointed out, "the therapist is ethically obligated to give the therapeutic benefits of treatment highest priority, independent of all other considerations."

The committee recognized that there are many situations creating dilemmas for the honest and ethical therapist, especially when concern for the health and care of the patient will require treatments which do not quite conform to the descriptions honored by the insurance provider. In these cases, the APTA warns, the tendency to bend the rules should always be limited. If a therapy can reasonably be defined or described using the insurance provider's terminology, fine. If not, "the use of such a description would be unethical." In effect, the general ethical duty of "truth-telling" is at work. Simply feeling that moral duty to the patient demands it, a physical therapist is not justified in falsifying records or breaking the law. The Code, the Guide, the Standards of Practice and the guidance by the committee all state that the therapist is responsible if therapy services are misused. When in doubt, other professional opinions should be sought, but ultimately, the therapist must take responsibility for decisions as to the application of therapy or treatment.

The APTA Code of Ethics and supplementary documents by the APTA can prove to be useful tools in court discussions of gray- area over-utilization. Since the Guide to Practice states at 3.3.C that treatment should be no more frequent than necessary for greatest improvement, and since the APTA itself indicates that a therapist should recommend discontinuing therapy when no gain is being made, these provisions can provide a compelling courtroom argument that excessive treatment, either in duration or frequency, violates the ethics of the profession. Of course, since the proper duration and frequency is difficult to establish with finality, proof of excess must still be made. A physical therapist can simply claim, that in his or her professional opinion, continued treatment was required. Yet the Code and the other APTA documents can provide the fundamental principles upon which the propriety of the discussion is based.

The APTA does not operate as do some professional associations (such as Bar Associations for Attorneys), by certifying or denying the right to practice to fellow professionals. Most Physical Therapists are not members of the APTA (only about a third are members), and membership or denial of membership would not affect their license to practice therapy. For those reasons, the ethics as established by the APTA can only serve as guidelines, and are not enforceable by the APTA itself. If the code is to prove useful as a tool to limit unethical behavior, it will have to be enforced through utilization review, claims denial, litigation of disputed cases, and possible license reviews before state boards.

Commentary

The continued overuse and abuse of physical therapy will only result in even further restrictions by insurance carriers on reimbursement with stricter utilization review and other cost-containment measures. We had better see the light soon.

Nathaniel Randolph
PT Bulletin, May 17, 1989

CHAPTER TWO ENDNOTES

1. Michael Schachner, "UR decisions can trigger liability suits," *Business Insurance*, October 2, 1989, p. 30.
2. Howard Larkin, "What used to be staff duty is now an extra; utilization review, special services earn some physicians a stipend," *American Medical News*, May 25, 1990 p. 17.
3. "Northwestern Bell takes home its medical review," *Employee Benefit Plan Review*, July 1988, p. 28; Norma R. Fritz, "Employers get wise to healthcare costs," *Personnel*, August, 1988, p. 17; Steve Taratella, "Utilization review cuts firm's health care costs. (Control Data Corp.)," *Business Insurance*, April 6, 1987, p. 22.
4. Wendall C. Harness, "Fraud costing insurers $16B annually," *National Underwriter Property & Casualty Risk-Bennefits Management*, September 18, 1989, p. 28; Robert P. Hey and Barbara Bradley, "450 billion industry spawns fraud, abuse. (Department of Health and Human Services, other agencies investigate health care industry)," *The Christian Science Monitor*, December 7, 1988, p. 1; "New Jersey care insurers investigated," *New York Times*, August 27, 1989, sec. 1 p. 14, 34.
5. The methods and limitations of applying the screens of HCFA are spelled out in "Documentation: The PT's Course on Successful Reimbursement," A Continuing Education Self-Study Course, by Carole Bernstein Lewis, sponsored by the Foundation for Physical Therapy, 1989.
6. Harris Meyer, "Delegates angered by growing review activity," *American Medical News*, 1990 (date, page.)
7. Michael M. Biehl and Linda M. Laarman, "Legal problems of health care cost containment," *Employment Relations Today*. Spring, 1988, p. 1.
8. Directory of utilization review vendors. (includes related information) (directory), *Business Insurance* February 19, 1990 p. 34; Linda Koco, "Programs" can turn into 'industries,'" *National Underwriter Life & Health*-Financial Services Edition, June 25, 1990, p. 31: Ellen Weisman, "UR oversight may ease provider woes," *Hospitals*, March 20, 1990, p. 82.
9. Joanne Wojcik, "Self Monitoring urged to let UR mature," *Business Insurance,* June 25, 1990, p. 20.
10. Harris Meyer,"Delegates angered to growing review activity." *American Medical News,* July 6, 1990, p. 6; Harris Meyer, "UR groups launch accreditation effort, ask AMA and insurers to join," *American Medical News*, March 2, 1990, p. 3; Christine Woolsey, "UR coalition promotes standards, accreditation," *Business Insurance,* February 19, 1990, p. 2; Donna DiBlase, "AMA to push uniform rules for UR firms," *Business Insurance*, January 22, 1990, p. 1; Carol Stevens, "Doctors are fighting back against bullying reviewers," *Medical Economics*, January 22, 1990, p. 25; Charles Culhane, "Utilization review valuable if done well - AMA," *American Medical News*, July 1, 1988, p. 3.
11. Martha Brannigan, "Courts rule both ways on 'pictures of pain,'" (usage of medical thermography is contested by insurance companies), *Wall Street Journal*, June 5, 1990, p. B1.
12. APTA Journal, 1986 {clipping not dated}/The Guide section cited is 3.3.C.

3 The Insurance Business

COST CONTAINMENT AND UTILIZATION REVIEW

Cost Containment: Practical Impediments
The Insurance Business
First Party, Second Party, Third Party
The Sentinel Effect as a Goal
Cost Containment as Social Policy
Cost Containment as a Good Business Policy
Barriers to Progress

COST CONTAINMENT: PRACTICAL IMPEDIMENTS

As an employee of the insurance company, the claims adjuster has to determine whether there is coverage, whether there is liability, and the amount and type of damages. While the insurance claims professional needs to apply as much thought to the medical issues in a claim as to the pure insurance issues, all too frequently, a number of factors work against such medical decisions. The claims professional more often than not finds it easier to pay the bills, rather than pursuing them.

Legal, practical, and administrative reasons are impediments to effective cost containment in the claims industry. Despite suspicious aspects of a case, it might be far easier, legally and in terms of company policy and workload, to simply write a check to pay for all the medical bills submitted.

The responsibility of an insurance company under the law is to correctly determine, in a timely manner, whether a claim is justified. The failure to decide promptly to pay reasonable and necessary costs can be regarded as bad faith, and open the insurance company to a costly suit. This obligation of the insurance company to meet its contract with its customer creates a pressure to move promptly and quickly to pay the bills.

Full investigation of medical bills is time consuming, and could delay payment of a legitimate charge. When the bills are questioned, more information is required: more copying of documentation is required; there may be a simple inconvenience factor in tracking down missing information, getting all the back-up documentation and information required from the therapists and other health care providers involved. Unexpected delays can easily mount up during an investigation. There is the need to interface with the insurance company's attorney, and the claimant's attorney, both of whom need to consult crowded schedules. It will take time to get all the needed reports; the adjuster will need to interpret the reports, which may be difficult to interpret or use; if reports costs money, those charges will be added to the file, or "expensed" to the file; if the adjuster does not know how to deal with a particular problem, the supervisor will be consulted. All of these immediate and practical matters serve as impediments to the practice of good cost containment.

Another common scenario, rooted in the persistence of corporate culture, works against effective cost containment. A young or energetic adjuster may see the problems in a case's medical bills, may know that there are ways of addressing those problems, and may begin to expend the effort to begin an investigation. The adjustor might decide to engage an outside reviewer or to bring in an outside expert. However, to get an outside report may require authority for the expenditure from a supervisor. The supervisor, having worked for years in the company, under the existing traditional corporate culture in which claims were rarely challenged, may simply say, "Pay the claim." Such a decision will defeat all the work and the drive that the adjuster has just expended to address the issues. In the 1990s, such patterns are common: many times the more senior supervisors do not believe in cost containment; they may remain unconvinced that the process will do any good. They see the problems with cost containment and utilization review, rather than seeing through the problems to the long range benefits. Unless the company has established a firm, management-backed policy, seeing through the problems and the expenses, to the need to establish a pattern, any individual eager adjuster becomes easily discouraged. "Why should I expend the effort and money on this file, when I am not going to get the support," the adjuster concludes, "when my supervisor says to go ahead and pay the bill?"

> *Commentary*
>
> *The companies have to get the consistent message out: "The days are gone where you submit a bill and a check is cut." The company must work to implant the thought that times have changed. They must let the attorneys know: "You can expect a challenge." They have to get the word out, but that takes time. You need to have a system set up to get the pattern. One of the problems with many carriers is that if they have cost-containment it is only applied to the most outrageous cases. They do not train their people; they don't even have the simplest guidelines or criteria such as identifying the "hot pack only" or "gaps in care" or the "palliative care" or the "exercise only" cases.*
>
> *Nathaniel Randolph*

In this chapter we look at some of the details of how the insurance industry is structured in the United States, and investigate in more depth some of the factors which work for and against the establishment of effective cost containment.

THE INSURANCE BUSINESS

In the United States, some smaller companies are very exclusive in that they write a "small book" or body of insurance, in some cases, only for a particular religious group; other companies work only with farmers or rural people, or serve customers in a particular small region of the nation. Some of these more exclusive companies experience very low levels of fraud or abuse; in effect, they count on the membership of the organization or the ethics or religious values of the insureds to provide a built-in means of cost containment. Such firms, however, have a very limited fraction of the total insurance business. Some more national companies attempt to restrict their automobile coverage by directing their marketing to the safest drivers, excluding drivers with poor records to the extent permitted by state law.

However, most of the liability insurance in the United States is carried by large, interstate firms, writing insurance for a wide population. Such firms are very inclusive, and sell insurance in almost every state, in urban and suburban communities, and have vast operations. For such companies, any effort at cost containment is complicated by the fact that the insurance business is under regulation by state laws with an insurance commission in each state and with great variation in types of coverage under state liability laws, with variations in court practices from state to state, and by the lack of a clear economic incentive to control costs.

Traditionally, if insurance companies could demonstrate that the cost of claims had increased, state commissions would allow for rate increases to cover, or partially cover, the increased costs. Whatever factors caused medical claims to increase in cost, whether general inflation, more active litigation, or the increasingly capital-intensive nature of medical treatment -- all would be passed on to the rate payer. As a consequence, the state commissions would allow the insurance companies to also pass on the cost of unexamined fraud, abuse, and over- utilization, directly to the rate-paying customers through higher premiums.

Through the 1980s, as the voters in state after state protested the cost of insurance, several states adopted different approaches to controlling that cost. In California, Proposition 103 resulted in a flat cap on insurance premiums; that system, while it had a simple appeal, like many simple solutions to complex problems, rapidly broke down. Other states, such as Pennsylvania, adopted systems of mandated peer-review coupled with a fee schedule to establish cost controls.

Through the 1990s, several currents converge to put limits on climbing insurance costs. State legislation under discussion in several states would set up a variety of mandated peer review and utilization review systems for casualty claims. Fee schedules, similar to those operative in the Accident and Health field will be established. Other states will try to control the cost of lawsuits by establishing "No-Fault" or "Assumed Risk" plans for cases under a certain dollar figure, or for certain categories of risk.

A few of the larger companies, recognizing gradually that cost-containment can reduce their climbing expenses and make them more competitive under state-regulated premium ceilings, have quietly initiated organized systems of cost containment through utilization review. For that reason, some companies will voluntarily adopt methods of cost-containment to improve their competitive position. All of these changes will result in internal upheaval inside many companies as the older culture of "Settle and Pay" gives way to "Review and Contain," whether by the force of law or through understanding of the business advantages of such a move. The guidelines provided in later chapters of this book will provide ideas, systems, and principles that may be adopted by those firms moving to cost containment.

FIRST PARTY, SECOND PARTY, THIRD PARTY

In insurance language, the "First Party" is the insured individual, the purchaser of the insurance; the "Second Party" is the insurance company; the "Third Party" is a claimant who has a claim against the first party's carrier. Thus when individuals, driving their own automobiles, collide with immovable objects and suffer injuries, they bring "First Party" claims to their own insurance companies. If an insured happened to run into another car and injure its driver, the driver of that car would bring a "Third Party" claim against the insured. The insurance company provides coverage against that claim under the insured's "BI" or Bodily Injury protection. Typically, BI insurance coverage pays for the insured driver's legal liability for bodily injury inflicted on someone else.

Some states offer "Med Pay" or medical payments in first party claims. Typically "Med Pay" sets low benefits and low limits on the injury claims, often with a maximum at $5000, unless the individual paid for extra coverage. MedPay coverage is designed to cover medical and funeral expenses of the driver, passengers, and pedestrians.

Other states have "PIP" or personal injury protection (with somewhat higher limits, sometimes offered optionally at higher premiums than the mandatory MedPay) commonly paid out in first party claims. PIP generally covers more than the MedPay plans: medical expenses, wage losses, funeral expenses, and rehabilitation and replacement services required by the injury. The payment in a first party injury is in the nature of the fulfillment of a contract: the insured individual has contracted with the company to pay premiums and in exchange to have the company pay reasonable and necessary medical costs to the limits described in the MedPay or the PIP coverage. The contractual nature of the first-party (insured) -second party (insurance company) relationship means that the insurance company is under a "Good Faith" obligation to fulfill a contract, backed up by the legal framework of contract law.

In Virginia, Maryland, Delaware, Georgia, and the District of Columbia among other states, an "Add-on" provision allows individual drivers to recover "in tort" those personal injury expenses which exceed the coverages under first party benefits available in their casualty insurance contracts. The term derives from the fact that such claims are added on to the tort coverage. The Add-on provision rules that the contract between the first and second party does not exclude lawsuits for claims which go beyond the limits provided in basic coverage.

The coverages under both PIP and MedPay vary from state to state in other ways. Some states also offer Uninsured Motorist (UM) and Underinsured Motorists (UIM) protections, which again, are defined by state law and vary in detail from state to state. In situations in which an individual has Uninsured Motorist coverage, some complex cases may arise. An individual can get coverage to the maximum under the MedPay or PIP coverage, and then can file, as a "third party" (against his or her own insurance company) for Uninsured or Underinsured Motorist if that kind of coverage was in place. The insurance company handles such a case as a contractual relationship for the MedPay or the PIP, and as "Claim" filed by a third party case, for the proportion of the accident which is covered under the Uninsured Motorist coverage. In this fashion, insurance consumers can have both first party cases and third party claims against their own insurance companies, a rather common, if tangled, occurrence in many jurisdictions. In practice, each is handled by a separate adjuster, and the files never meet, even though it is the same person filing the claim.

First party cases, within the prescribed limits, when not encumbered by Add-on provisions or by Uninsured Motorist clauses, were traditionally fairly clear cut, and paid without difficulty. The reasons for this pattern are several. A charge of "Bad faith" brought by an individual against an insurance company to the insurance commissioner in a state would cause severe problems. Judges and juries, if brought into a case, might tend to sympathize with an individual who had paid all bills, contracted for coverage, and then had been denied that coverage, assuming that the bills for care seemed logical, reasonable, and necessary. A judge and a jury, in cases of reasonableness or necessity which could be interpreted either way, might suspect the insurance company of not living up, in good faith, to the obligations of its contract with the insured. Under such pressures, companies would often react to first party claims as straightforward bills to be paid, once coverage and liability had been established.

Insurance firms and peer reviewers discover abuses and bills that have been "run up" in both First Party and Third Party cases. For example, a health care provider, in a first party case, has every incentive to run up the bill to the maximum limit set by what they might see as the "pool" of money in the MedPay or PIP coverage. "Attorney-directed" care is more likely in third party cases, in which the attorney is hoping to develop a large claim, based upon a variety of medical bills as well as loss of earnings to the client. Thus the motivation for abuse exists in both first and third party cases.

Insurance firms encounter attorneys representing the health care providers in first party cases; in third party cases, it is more common for the claimant or injured party to be represented by an attorney. In Add-on states, insurance companies will also encounter attorneys representing first-party claimants, who have claims which exceed the basic MedPay or PIP coverage and are suing their own companies under the Add-on provision; and as we have discussed, some cases can shift from first party to third party under Uninsured Motorist coverage, complicating the picture.

In some states, if an insurance company shows bad faith in a first party case, the potential damages are unlimited. In one case in Georgia, when a company refused to pay a first party claim of $750, the insured won an award of over $1,000,000 after demonstrating bad faith. Each state has a "Unfair Claims Settlement Practices Act," or similarly-titled legislation governing the contractual relationship in insurance situations, defining and controlling what constitutes bad faith. A violation of the act often is punishable by a fine, and a conviction under the act can open a punitive damages case on the grounds of malice. Under those claims acts, for an insurance company to reject a first party claim and at the same time to protect itself against charges that it has practiced bad faith, the company must prove that the care provided or the bills submitted were not "reasonable and necessary." Faced with the possibility of "bad faith" suits in such jurisdictions, which not only are potentially expensive, but which create a negative public image likely to damage a company's competitive position, a carrier has very good reasons not to be as agressive in its utilization review and its cost containment on first party as it might be on third party cases.

In a third party situation, the bills are not presented against a contract, but as a claim, which is negotiable. In effect there is no dollar limit in third party claims, providing the claimant and the attorney with an incentive to build up the claim as high as possible. The injured third party's attorney presents a "demand," which may be as much as the attorney thinks represents a good bargaining position. Theoretically, it may be based on a multiple of three or four times the total of the medical payments, the loss of income, and the property damage, with the multiple representing a factor for pain and suffering. Commonly, however, a demand for as much as $75,000 may be settled for less than $10,000.

A plaintiff's attorney may decide to drop a case, or settle for the amount offered. Knowing that the carrier may go to court, the plaintiff's attorney has to decide whether it is worth the time and trouble and may advise the client to accept the offer or to fight and possibly lose. Commonly, the plaintiff's attorneys want to settle out of court because, from their point of view, more money can be made in the less time-consuming process of negotiated settlement than in more protracted courtroom proceedings.

So, while one might expect the third party cases to be more often fought out in court, due to the high amounts involved and the contentious nature of claims for damages, the vast majority of such cases never make it to court. In the late 1980s, statistics revealed that less than 3 per cent of all cases filed actually went to court. The reason that only a small proportion were brought to trial is the weighing of profit motives by attorneys and clients. Nevertheless, a reasonable and objective social policy might point to negotiation as cheaper than litigation; if both parties are dealing with the same set of objective facts, a reasonable agreement should be struck which will reduce the social cost of trials. Many jurisdictions encourage negotiated settlement rather than trial for just that reason. States which have experimented with No-Fault insurance systems for various aspects of automobile accident risks have aimed at reducing the cost of litigation by handling most small cases, regardless of who was legally at fault in an accident, as first-party claims between the insureds and their own companies.

State legislation governs all of these arrangements. A survey of the 50 states and the District of Columbia conducted in 1987 revealed the following:

NO-FAULT. Fourteen states restricted the right to sue for minor auto injury claims; insurance provided substantial Personal Injury Protection (PIP) regardless of whose fault the accident was. The laws had various "tort thresholds"--expense limits above which an injury would qualify for a lawsuit or liability claim against the driver at fault.

ADD-ON. Eleven states allowed suits beyond PIP; some of these states made PIP coverage mandatory, others made it optional.

TORT LIABILITY. Twenty six states retained traditional tort liability systems, requiring proof of negligence against a driver, and liability claims against that driver. These states allowed MED-PAY coverage to provide for no-fault coverage of the driver, passengers, and sometimes, pedestrians. But third party claims would be brought against the insured's BI policy.[1]

With such variation state to state, it is difficult to offer generalizations about insurance practice which hold true on a national basis. However, there are several patterns. Those companies which are moving to utilization review and to cost containment actually use expert testimony in court more often in first party cases than in third party cases. Such testimony begins the process of public education, starting first with judges and juries, creating a more general awareness of abusive practices. Denial of excessive or padded bills in first party cases often put the "good name" of the insurance company on trial against the reputation of the health care provider. In those cases, the company must defend its decision that a bill was not reasonable or necessary, and that it was therefore not under a contractual obligation to pay the bills. When proving a point regarding necessity or reasonableness of care, the company must demonstrate that the health care provider and/or the patient were engaged in a useless, wasteful, fraudulent, or near-fraudulent practice. Particularly in those cases where the fraud or abuse can be traced to an unscrupulous health-care provider, the insurance company will require the services of peer-reviewers, expert witnesses, independent medical examiners, and sometimes, outside credible utilization review experts.

Most auto injuries are relatively minor. The 1987 study cited above revealed that 43% of BI claims in tort states and 43% of PIP claims in no-fault states involved losses less than $500. However, a small number of expensive claims, representing only 4 to 6% of the cases, were over $10,000, and accounted for large proportions of the total paid out. The study noted vastly increased costs of automobile claims between 1977 and 1987: the average BI claim increased from $3376 to $8074 over that period, while the average no-fault PIP claim increased from $999 to $2538. The increase could be traced to two causes: higher medical bills, and more attorney involvement. The study attributed the increase in attorney involvement to the sheer increase in numbers of attorneys in practice, and to the 1978 Supreme Court ruling which allowed attorney advertising.[2]

The national study also revealed that no-fault insurance systems had done little to control attorney involvement or escalating costs. A surprising number of cases in no-fault states exceeded the limits of the no-fault coverage, and involved lawsuit, or attorney-directed negotiation. For example, over 60% of persons receiving PIP benefits in New Jersey could successfully file for a BI tort claim for amounts exceeding the threshold.[3]

THE SENTINEL EFFECT AS A GOAL

Companies that are serious about cost containment must establish a structured program in all of their claims offices. If they do it properly, the insurance company can deliver a clear message to the provider community and to the plaintiffs' bar that there is a strong likelihood that when medical bills are submitted, they are going to be subject to some scrutiny. The companies need to implant the thought with the providers -- "The days are gone, when you submit a bill and a check is cut without question." That message will create a "Sentinel Effect," a policy which stands like a sentinel discouraging the unscrupulous from attempting to raid the treasury of insurance reserves.

In order for claims review and cost containment to have the Sentinel Effect, medical practitioners and the plaintiff's bar have to come to recognize that a particular insurance company is serious about controlling fraud, abuse, and simple over-utilization. That realization will only come if the system of cost-containment is consistent. A random, hit-or-miss identification of an occasional abusive or over-utilization claim may be psychologically rewarding to the adjuster involved, but unless it represents part of a pattern, an isolated denial of an extreme claim will not discourage unscrupulous claimants.

For cost containment to work, adjusters need to apply the same thoroughness to the "medical specials" as they do to the other, insurance aspects of a claim. By "medical specials" the adjuster refers to all of those expenses connected to the medical side of the case: bills for diagnostic testing; for consultations; for examinations; for therapy sessions. The term is a catch-all phrase for all the medical bills that have been incurred in a claim. Some health care providers will order extra tests and pass the patient around to other providers for consultations, the "ping-ponging" effect which is discussed in chapter three. When an attorney is directing the provision of healthcare, often the patient is directed to get more treatment and examination than may be necessary. Thus, it is often that the "Medical Specials" side of the file literally becomes the "fat side" of the folder, providing a simple and vivid indication of a need for review. But the Sentinel Effect must grow out of more than the simple reaction of an adjuster to the suspicious nature or the fat wad of paper represented in the medical specials.

In order to establish an effective cost containment program, insurance claims departments need to establish well-thought out check-lists, criteria, and guidelines for the medical specials. Adjusters have checklists and criteria for the more mechanical and cut-and-tried aspects of the case, such as existence of coverage, type of coverage, exclusions, whether or not the insurance is paid up, and the valuation of property damage. The examination of the medical specials must be conducted with the same logic and clarity. Suggested guidelines for such an approach are provided in Chapter 5 of this work.

Traditionally, courts and juries look on the claims by first parties much more favorably than they do third parties. Nevertheless, as the Sentinel Effect of close claims review takes hold for a few firms, some courts are becoming more sympathetic to the insurance companies. Good expert testimony has repeatedly demonstrated that it is not always necessary to pay a bill simply because it was presented. The Sentinel Effect is a learning process on the part of judges and juries.

Insurance carriers that are adopting cost containment with hopes of establishing a Sentinel Effect, are careful to pick and choose the cases that they go to court with. The carriers need to put attorneys and providers on notice that the old ways are changing. Selecting cases for denial is not simply a matter of deciding that the Medical Specials in a file are too thick. Rather, the policy decision of picking out cases for challenge has to be made at a high management and legal level in a firm, and reflect solid cases of one or another type of abuse, waste, fraud, or unethical practice on the part of the practitioner or the patient, or both. The more advanced companies in this area are choosing cases they think they can win, and cases in which there are obvious and clear-cut illustrations of different types of over-use.

Defense attorneys have to be involved in the strategic decisions as to which cases to reject, and which to defend in court. And in order to participate intelligently in working out a successful strategy, defense attorneys, whether in the employ of the carrier or on retainer to the carrier, have to be schooled and understand the medical issues and the defensibility of those issues. Not only must the attorney fully understand the issues in the case, but the attorney must believe firmly that the carrier's case is supportable in order to represent the firm in its best light. Just as in the case of plaintiffs' attorneys, many retained or in-house attorneys often would rather negotiate rather than go to trial, simply because negotiation might represent less work than preparing a trial case. They, like the adjusters and top management, must see their actions as part of a larger reform effort to put an end to the abuses of the accident game.

COST CONTAINMENT AS SOCIAL POLICY

In November 1990, a special Governor's Commission on Insurance in Maryland studied the causes of increases in automobile insurance premiums. In general, the study found, "increases in rates were driven by increases in loss cost or pure premium," not by decreased efficiency of the carriers. Because the insurance companies sought to remain competitive, they did not increase their rates as much as their costs, but asked for slightly smaller increases. To an extent, the companies were able to offset part of the loss from the difference between their increased costs and their smaller increase of rates, by obtaining slightly higher interest rates earned on the capital reserves which they held for payment of costs.

Because of their need to cover costs, insurance companies tend to loose money on the automobile part of their coverages. The study found that in 1988, for every $1 of auto liability premium, 73 cents went to losses, 12 cents went to pay for attorney fees and adjustment costs, and 22 cents went to company expenses. It will be noted that these three amounts add up to $1.07, leaving a 7 cent "underwriting" loss as the cost of doing automobile insurance business. Over a five year period, the average underwriting loss was 18 percent of premium.

Sixty percent of the loss dollars are paid out for items such as "pain and suffering," and forty percent for economic losses such as medical costs and lost wages. Nationwide, the severity of automobile accident claims continued to increase drastically, from an average in 1985 of $5,313 to an average of $7,645 in 1990, or an increase of 44 percent in 5 years.

That increase in severity of claim, the study found, derived from inflation in the health care sector, increased limits of coverage purchased, increased attorney representation, and what the study called "social" inflation. That last factor is the increased propensity of judges and juries to expand the liability beyond the scope that was considered when the policy was priced, combined with the increase in the size of awards for noneconomic losses such as pain and suffering. In short, a key factor in the rise of cost was not any tendency on the part of companies to take a higher rate of profit; rather the cost derived from increases in medical payments. Insurance companies distributed that cost to the locales which had the highest claim rates and highest accident rates, accounting for the extremely high premiums in urban areas. Overall, the urban driver paid more than double the premium charged in rural areas.[4]

In order to achieve cost containment some companies attempt to establish in-house standards; others work with utilization review firms, some with a computer-based method of sorting and identifying the cases more likely to benefit from close examination; still others combine those techniques with outside consultants. Whatever approach they employ, the more competitive firms will need to move to a structured and organized system of cost-containment and utilization review if they are to survive in the 1990s.

In the past, fee schedules, peer review, and provider recourse were established in the areas of Accident and Health, and such concepts were unheard of in liability cases. The casualty side of the insurance business traditionally said, "You bill, we pay." But the public, and through the public, legislatures, have demanded that some of the efforts to establish cost control in Accident and Health be applied to the skyrocketing liability issues. Things are changing rapidly. The number of utilization review firms serving casualty insurers in the United States has grown from zero in 1980, to 200 in 1989, to over 400 companies by 1991. Now that peer review organizations are working on the casualty side of insurance as well as on the accident and health side, some state agencies are becoming involved in regulating them, and moving to establish fixed fee schedules which apply to casualty cases.

In Pennsylvania, Act 6 not only established a fee schedule, to pay first party benefits, but also stated that peer review was mandated. The law spelled out who could do peer review, and set up a system for health providers' recourse in disputed cases. Utilization review firms had to be certified by the state in order to perform reviews. As a consequence of the law, within a year, many of the most abusive health providers in that state found themselves seriously challenged.

Some states have started to regulate utilization review companies, setting up systems of accreditation, while other states, in 1991, are considering such regulatory legislation. The American Managed Care and Review Association (AMCRA) has worked on self-policing by utilization review firms, has followed closely state law changes affecting ability of review firms to do business in different states, and has supported the work of the Utilization Review Accreditation Commission (URAC) to establish national utilization review standards. In November, 1990, URAC issued its draft standards for comment. The standards spelled out such items as: the kinds of information upon which review should be based; the necessity for written procedures and prompt handling; procedures for appeal of decisions by both patients and health care providers; confidentiality of records; a standard requiring that reviews of work by licensed health professionals be conducted by individuals licensed to practice the same medical service; and procedures for conducting reviews in hospitals.[5]

The various systems of accreditation, regulation, and self- policing need to be fully worked out in order to protect insurance companies which use utilization review from "bad faith" charges. If a claimant could demonstrate in court that an insurance company subjected the claim to outside review simply in order to get a certain proportion of its claims rejected, the whole utilization review principle could be severely damaged. If the courts ruled that a utilization review firm was simply a "hired gun" employed to reject cases, the whole procedure would fail. Thus self-policing and accreditation are essential.

In 1991, AMCRA collected information on a state by state basis to determine the status of legislation regulating utilization review firms. The January, 1991 review revealed several cross-currents in legislation. In several states, medical professionals had lobbied to prevent the extension of utilization review or to severely limit the activity. In some states, concerns with cost containment had driven efforts to establish clear cut licensing and accreditation procedures to guarantee that utilization review be conducted fairly. A few states had worked to prevent out-of-state review firms from operating within their state. Other states were simply gathering data, conducting surveys, or working towards a system of voluntary standards, and in some states, no action at all had been reported. The rapidly- changing picture in early 1991 gave an indication that further dramatic changes in the growth of utilization review would be likely to dominate the 1990s.

On the one hand, legislators concerned with health care cost containment hoped to establish systems of control. Organized physicians, hospitals, and other health-care groups tended to lobby against utilization review. States considering some system of utilization review were concerned over such issues as protecting the legitimate patient, guaranteeing good-faith contract compliance by insurance companies, and making sure that any system of utilization review be conducted professionally. The self-policing standards of URAC were a step in the direction of assuring states that the system could be fair to all concerned; in the case of the District of Columbia, URAC standards were under consideration for official adoption by the District.[6]

> *Commentary*
>
> *When the insurance companies wise up to cost containment, that will keep the phony claims out. In the meantime, the problem is training adjusters and attorneys to become familiar with the issues, especially in the physical therapy over-use area.*
>
> *Nathaniel Randolph*

COST CONTAINMENT AS GOOD BUSINESS PRACTICE

In the 1990s, a few of the larger and more forward looking insurance companies in the casualty business were getting very serious about cost containment, and were implementing new procedures on a company - wide, national basis. Even in these firms, however, the cultural shift was difficult and the new policy ran into severe internal politics. Staff raised on the older values continued to see the problem as a tough choice, between happy customers on the one hand, and cost containment on the other. Firms found it difficult to build in new incentives for the claims individual to save money. If a company were to set a policy of quotas or budget incentives to reduce claims and to set that as a policy, that fact would constitute grounds for first party "Bad Faith" claims. Yet without a company-wide policy, the individual claims adjuster has every incentive not to adopt cost containment. Many would see any close review process, adopted unilaterally, as only creating more work. A supervisor will look at the number of "pendings" or open files on the adjuster's desk, measuring progress through claims in a strict numerical fashion. There is always pressure, some of it from the supervisor, some from the adjuster, to close the files. The problem is, if an adjuster starts a review process, even more open files, more pendings, will pile up on the desk, because of the fact that the review simply takes time. And every utilization review consultation, every involvement of peer review, every independent medical examination or request for further paperwork will result in "expensing" the file.

Another incentive to move claims out, rather than reviewing them, is that when a claim is paid, the expense does not come out of the department's budget; rather out of claims reserves. Yet if further manpower is needed by a claims department to increase review, that cost will require stretching manpower and budget further. So, from a bureaucratic point of view, it is difficult to implement a cost containment system simply in one claims office or in one region, unless the policy has the support of central management. In some small, but clearly abusive cases, the cost of the bill submitted would be considerably less than the cost of investigation, expert witnesses, and litigation expenses. The cost-benefit analysis in such a situation must be made at the highest level of the firm, and represent a commitment to the concept, that in the long run, the Sentinel Effect will save costs and reduce the underwriting cost.

If the company sets up the correct spirit and attitude as a company-wide policy, in which cost containment and solid claims review is adopted, it will show benefit to the whole company. One national firm found that, with a good peer-review and utilization review policy, instead of claims costs rising at 20 per cent per year, the increase was cut to 7 per cent year, within the range of the general cost of living. That result got the corporate leadership to sit up and take notice, and to give support to the concept.

The wave of the future will be that cost containment advocates will not only convince top management, they will aggressively carry the benefits to the general public in the form of a public relations campaign. Just as a few carriers have won support by providing police departments with radar equipment and families with baby-restraint systems for their cars, to show that they are serious about safety and concerned to reduce casualties, so they may soon prove that they are serious about controlling premiums and medical costs by employing cost containment. If an insurance company can prove to its customers that it holds their rates down by preventing them from paying for unnecessary, unreasonable, fraudulent, or falsely padded claims, the false claims against that particular firm would decline, and the customer base would increase. Cost containment will be a public relations bonanza, once the companies understand it and convey to their customers.

> *Commentary*
> *Once companies wise up to cost containment, they will have such a reduction in the amount of care allowed and the amount billed, most of the cases won't even get to court.*
> *Nathaniel Randolph*

Some of the larger corporations that are self-insured have already adopted a primitive means of patient-regulated cost containment. The employer tells the employee to look at a medical bill, and to identify any false charges, or treatments that they did not receive. The employee is promised a proportion of all funds saved through denial of claims. Some labor unions which have worked out health plans also have similar programs. Such concepts, in the interest of both the employer and the employee, provide the simplest kind of self-audit or review of the billing process and allow patients to become their own cost containment claims reviewers.

BARRIERS TO PROGRESS

For insurance companies to fully realize the benefits of cost-containment, they must set up systems in which the claims adjusters apply the same energy and emphasis to medicals as to the rest of the file. The barriers to establishing this emphasis run deep. Some are widespread in American society. Insurance companies are captured by tradition and history in patterns; the old culture of "Pay the Bills, Move the claims," is pervasive. And at the level of individual claims personnel, it is often easier to do nothing.

To some extent, it is the national mentality, prevalent in the sixties and declining somewhat through the 1980s, which set the tone. Americans had a kind of confidence in both money and technology, with the attitude that if you spend enough on the problem, you find the solution. By such values, paying more for health care seemed logical. Through the post war decades, hundreds of hospitals were built with Hill-Burton funds. Coupled with the concept that health care, like other problems, could be improved with more money, was the concept that new technology offered quick fixes and simple solutions. Equipment manufacturers understood this motivation, and sold machines of all kinds to doctors and physical therapists, with the argument that a provider could increase revenues well into the six-figure range, and that the patients would also benefit, from the new, capital-intensive equipment. All of these issues fed the system. Furthermore, the American people sometimes tend to use paid medical care, not necessarily because they need it, but because it is viewed as an "entitlement." Scandals have arisen over the over-prescription of pacemakers; Americans are notorious for taking both prescription drugs and over-the counter nostrums. So when one looks for the root causes of the rise of medical costs, one should not blame just the companies, but look to American values and ideals, to the attitudes that money and technology will solve problems, and that whatever the doctor orders is likely to make you feel better.

As we have seen, the question of extending the benefits of peer review and utilization review from accident and health insurance to casualty insurance is subject to the laws of the 50 states and the District of Columbia. Provisions in the state's Fair Claims Practices Acts may prevent wholesale adoption of utilization review without clarifying legislation. Organized political lobbying and resistance by Plaintiff attorneys and by health care providers to any measures likely to limit awards effectively prevents extension of utilization review procedures in some jurisdictions.

Other barriers to change exist at the level of the insurance companies. As we have seen, they too were captured by the values which dominated America, and for years, they found they had an easy ride. If costs went up, if claims increased, the volume of business would increase and the rate-payers would ultimately pick up the tab. Paying claims reflected the burden of tradition, of history--that was the way it was always done. A claim came in. The insurance checklist was examined closely. If coverage existed, the adjusters would move the claim out and pay the bill. Insurance professionals who developed their work habits and their values in that context naturally would find it difficult to change, simply because of the force of corporate culture expressed in habit, tradition, values, and training. For such reasons, part of the blame for the barrier to progress in cost containment has to go back to the insurance companies who never looked closely at what they did. Once in a while an abuse would be checked, but the approach was sporadic, not systematized. It was easier to pay, and the companies paid for abuse after abuse.

Thus at the level of those who abuse the system--a few unscrupulous health practitioners and attorneys--the easy flow of money created a pattern. This system of only casual or intermittent attempts to examine claims said to the physical therapist and to the other providers, "stack up the modalities, run up the bills." After all, they had good reason to believe, the insurance companies will pay for whatever you put down. Similarly, the incentive was there for attorneys, who would pile up stacks of cases and negotiate for generous settlements.

The companies, everyone thought, had "Deep Pockets." The obvious fact that those pockets were indeed the pockets of the average consumer, the average rate payer, who provided out of increased insurance bills, the billions of wasted dollars, seemed easy to forget. Millions of people paid higher insurance bills, and thought of it as simply another aspect of inflation, not realizing that the insurance rate went up by a percentage that was twice to four times the cost of living increase through the 1980s. The average citizen paid for abuse by the few.

By believing that it was the wealthy insurance companies who paid for the bills, juries were willing to award large claims, and to sympathize with "the little guy," against the huge company. Because most insurance companies have not cared, have been sloppy in their practices, and because they have not taken the leadership in explaining that the escalation was partially based on fraud, abuse, and over-utilization, the companies for years abdicated their responsibility.

But there were signs in the late 1980s and the 1990s that the people were beginning to wake up to the issues, despite the fact that the market system failed to provide incentives for change. The California voters, with Proposition 103 simply put a ceiling on rates, an unworkable system, but reflective of the growing popular discontent. A reform minded approach, as in Pennsylvania, forced peer review and the beginnings of a system of cost containment. Yet politically-expressed concern on the part of consumers over cost containment will continue to lead to study after study, legislative battle after battle; and more states will move to control the abuses in various ways.

As state legislatures and insurance companies woke up to the levels of abuse and costs which could be controlled by close utilization review, two forces would work together to overcome the barriers of cultural and institutional inertia. On the one hand, as consumers recognize that the companies' deep pockets are their own, they will be more supportive of firms which work to control costs. As state legislatures seek ways to control cost and as they seek to certify and license competent utilization reviewers, they will impose systems which provide incentives and provide requirements for control. And, as those cost-control measures spread, the competitive possibilities in a systematic cost containment approach will be realized by the more aggressive and forward looking companies. As they change and get a better share of the market, the more traditional and slower moving insurance companies will have to follow suit or fall by the wayside. Together, these forces can create the Sentinel Effect, reducing the amount of abusive claims and bringing claims to reasonable and necessary levels.

CHAPTER THREE ENDNOTES

1. "Compensation for Automobile Injuries in the United States" (All-Industry Research Advisory Council, March 1989.) AIRAC, 100 Harger Road, Suite 310, Oak Brook, Illinois, 60521. Survey data presented on p. 3.
2. AIRAC study, p. 7, 9.
3. Ibid., 13.
4. Governor's Commission on Insurances, "Study of Private Passenger Automobile Liability Insurance System," November, 1990. (Prepared by Tillinghast Management Consultants and Actuaries.
5. The URAC standards are summarized from Utilization Review Accreditation Comission, "National Utilization Review Standards," November, 1990, issued by the URAC Standards Subcommittee, 1227 25th Street, N.W., Suite 610, Washington DC. 20037.
6. This information is compiled from the AMCRA Utilization Review Section, "State Legislative Update," January 29, 1991. This document is issued by the Government Affairs section of AMCRA, headquartered in Washington, D.C.

4. Documentation

Documents as the Crucial Link for Cost Containment
The Need for Objectivity
The "SOAP" Format
Elements of Good Documentation
The Referral
The Initial Report
Progress Notes
Discharge Reports
Billing Statements and Procedures
Evaluating Claim Documentation
22 Point Claims Review Checklist
Items to be Reviewed and Checked
A Final Word

DOCUMENTS AS THE CRUCIAL LINK FOR COST CONTAINMENT

In these days of spiraling health care costs, health care insurers are hard pressed to establish, follow, and enforce equitable reimbursement policies. Insurance adjusters and claims reviewers examine and reject more and more poorly documented claims. Nevertheless, it is still quite common for health care providers to submit claims with incomplete, poorly executed, or in some cases non-existent supportive documentation. As insurers work to establish cost containment through the Sentinel Effect, close examination of the documentation becomes the crucial link.

In 1987, a General Accounting Office [GAO] report on Medicare claims for rehabilitation services dramatically underscored the problem of inadequate or improper documentation. Of over 1100 cases and supporting materials studied, the GAO found that sixty-seven percent included documentation that was incomplete, vague, or otherwise lacking sufficient information to determine the claimant's eligibility. The GAO estimated that over a two-year period, Medicare paid over $50 million for inadequately supported claims. The GAO concluded with the recommendation that the Health Care Financing Administration [HCFA], the agency that administers Medicare, establish and strictly enforce guidelines for documentation required with physical therapy claims.[1]

Documentation for physical therapy serves many purposes beyond reimbursement. Docu-mentation primarily serves the therapist and the patient. Documentation identifies the major problems of the patient to be addressed by the physical therapy treatment, establishes a baseline for measuring patient progress, and indicates treatment effectiveness or treatment modification in managing the patient's symptoms. Documentation is the tool that allows for effective communication between health professionals and establishes the validity of the care provided.

Commentary

The role of documentation for the purposes of research cannot be overemphasized. It is unfortunate that physical therapy, as a profession, has until only recently not required or encouraged research to the extent seen in other professional disciplines. There is a lack of professional literature in the field, especially of basic research and writing, that could help to objectify procedures.

Because of its failure to produce much in the way of research, a great many of the problems associated with physical therapy billing are the fault of the profession. The APTA has attempted to establish standards of practice for physical therapy, but they are rather general and vague. The fact that there are no diagnosis-based standards is a serious problem. The main difficulty, however, in any attempt to establish diagnosis-based standards is the lack of research and a body of professional literature to draw upon. We can say that twenty weeks of therapy for a soft tissue injury is too much, but where is the research to substantiate that judgment? That is why so much now is left to the subjective professional judgment of the individual, and that is the fault of the profession.

Nathaniel Randolph

In the hospital setting, communication through progress notes allows members of the health care team to better coordinate their individual aspects of the patient's treatment. Responses to new medications or routines can be noted and acted upon more effectively in an open, cooperative environment. Moreover, accurate, objective progress notes can provide raw material for research, increasing the body of literature in the field of physical therapy, establishing criteria and standards for treatment, and providing further grist for the educational mill. From the point of view of the reimbursing party, however, documentation is the primary guide to the quantity, frequency, and appropriateness of therapy. As the legal record of patient treatment and outcomes, documentation provides the basic data to substantiate claims.

THE NEED FOR OBJECTIVITY

When documentation is provided, one often finds that the doctor or physical therapist has merely recorded subjective complaints, such as stiffness or achiness, reported by the patient as the basis for extensive physical therapy treatment. He or she often fails to provide the objectivity in testing and reporting that is the necessary grounding of sound patient care.

Objective tests, such as Range of Motion [ROM] or of strength or functional ability, result in findings that are reproducible and measurable. Yet patients often continue to receive treatment for what amounts to only subjective, and therefore unverifiable, complaints. Aside from the vague, subjective notations of pain or stiffness, there is often no indication of any type of impairment or disability requiring treatment.

In order to determine whether care is reasonable and necessary, it is useful to have a set of diagnostic methods which are objective. If an objective test reveals to several practitioners that the same treatment or therapy is desirable, such as range of motion or strengthening exercises, then we have a solid measure of the reasonableness and necessity of the treatment. Thus, objective testing noted in the record can be a valuable guide. In physical therapy, however, the defining line between subjective and objective testing is not always clear. Some tests are clearly objective, while others are clearly subjective, and still others, although subjective in quality, have an objective appearance or leave an impression of objectivity. Unless clearly documented, the results of many tests and evaluations will be so subjective that they provide very poor evidence of the need for therapy, or evidence of progress under therapy.

Even a measurable test such as "Active Range of Motion" [AROM] is subject to this problem. The therapist will ask the patient to raise his arm from his side to as far over his head as possible. If he can raise his arm to vertical with the floor, this could be objectively measured at 180 degrees, and a lesser measurement could indicate possible limitation. But the subjective element is that the patient limits his range of motion because of discomfort. A patient who stops at 150 degrees because it begins to hurt at that point is making a subjective judgment; another patient with the same injury might be able to tolerate moving his arm to the full vertical position.

Thus Passive Range of Motion [PROM] has more likelihood of representing an objective measure of the same problem. In a passive range test, the therapist will move the patient's limb through the range of motion, and will note where pain or an obstruction stops the motion. If pain stops the motion, again, the judgment is subjective; the therapist notes if there is a restriction, or a restriction with pain.

Commentary

While the SCALES method of measuring pain is a laudable first step toward achieving the goal of objectivity in documentation, it still relies too heavily on subjective assessment by the patient. I often see, when reviewing notes, a level of pain reported as an eight on a scale of one to ten. This type of report is difficult to take seriously. I cannot realistically conceive of anyone who is going to seek or receive care who would describe their level of pain as less than seven.

Nathaniel Randolph

When a therapist notes "tenderness" in a certain area, or if the patient complains of tenderness, the term can be a flag that a subjective standard was applied. On the other hand, a carefully described tenderness at a trigger point, or a lack of sensitivity to touch or to a pin prick at a point can be an objective measurement. Similarly, the test of the knee reflex, a neurological test, can be an objective measure of impairment.

A patient's complaint that he can no longer hold a certain tool or conduct a certain function, " a functional limitation" can be noted and will represent an objective finding. Similarly, impairment of regular day-to-day activities, such as dressing, tying shoes, and other Activities of Daily Living [ADLs] can be determined and objectively noted.

The practice of physical therapy is primarily involved in the restoration of function. While easing pain is an important objective of physical therapy, it is primarily to the extent that the pain causes a functional problem. Pain from an injury, for example, may prevent a patient from performing ordinary day-to-day activities and impact on his or her ability to perform on the job. A secretary, for example, who is unable to sit for long periods of time without pain, or a mailman who is unable to comfortably walk long distances, are two examples of functionally inhibiting pain. So while physical therapists do treat pain, they do (or should do) so with the sharper focus of removing any functional limitation resulting from the pain.

Some tests yield explicit, objective information. Clearly, records of vital signs, such as blood pressure and pulse rate are objective. Posture and gait analysis, with clear descriptions of problems, can be objective. A description such as "lordosis", indicating a posture with the pelvis canted forward, or "kyphosis" a "hunchback" position with the neck and head forward, are objective statements about a patient's posture but not necessarily problems.

THE "SOAP" FORMAT

Dr. Lawrence Weed introduced the concept of the problem- oriented clinical note at the University of Vermont in 1969. Since that time, the ideas put forward by Dr. Weed have become generally regarded as an ideal format for progress notes in many hospitals, medical schools, and rehabilitative settings.

Unlike the traditional narrative style note, the problem-oriented clinical note utilizes an outline format. There are five key elements to the problem-oriented clinical note:

    I. PROBLEM. The problem element refers to the condition for which the patient was originally referred for treatment. This may merely restate the physicians diagnosis, such as "tear of the medial collateral ligament," or it may relate the patient's chief complaint, such as "severe knee pain."

II. SUBJECTIVE INFORMATION. Subjective information is that which cannot be immediately confirmed by the patient's medical record. It may include relevant aspects of his/her medical history and the patient's own description of the condition which led him to seek therapy.

III. OBJECTIVE INFORMATION. This portion of the note contains information that is verifiable either from the patient's medical record or from testing conducted by the therapist or physician. This might cover such measurable aspects as range of motion, strength, joint stability, swelling, atrophy, and functional performance.

IV. ASSESSMENT. This section contains the therapist's interpretation of the information recorded in the objective section. The problems of the patient are identified and the goals of treatment are established.

V. PLAN. This section describes the proposed plan of treatment, to achieve the stated goals, the advisability of further tests, if the patient is to be referred to other departments, and the suggested frequency and duration of the treatment.

While similar material would be contained in anywell-structured note, regardless of style, the problem-oriented clinical note format has several advantages over the narrative style. The structure of the format lends itself easily to the adoption of a standard both intellectually and stylistically. It is easily readable, since important aspects of a patient's treatment can be viewed at a glance rather than requiring line- by-line interpretation as in a traditional narrative note. Finally, its format invites a disciplined approach to clinical note-taking.[2]

ELEMENTS OF GOOD DOCUMENTATION

As the insurance claims reviewer examines case files, he or she needs to be well aware of the standards of good documentation and should be alert for signs, through poor documentation, that therapy was either incorrectly billed, was unneeded, or was inappropriate. In addition to billing material, a complete documentation packet could include evidence of a referral from the attending physician, periodic reevaluations or recertifications by the physician, and complete initial, follow- up, reevaluation, daily progress notes, and discharge reports from the physical therapist. In those jurisdictions which do not permit direct access by the patient to the therapist, referral from the physician or other medical professional should be clearly documented.

According to Henry C. Wessman, M.S., progress notes "should tell the complete clinical story of the patient from admission to discharge." Each patient treatment should be documented and signed by the treating therapist on the date of each visit.

Many professionals believe that the progress note writer's ABC's should be "accuracy, brevity, and clarity." Objectivity should be the goal in recording tests and observations. Medical jargon, slang, or otherwise ambiguous wording and abbreviations should be avoided. Many times, notated diagrams convey meaning more easily than text. As progress notes sometimes become legal documents, they should always be recorded in ink, with the date and full signature of the physical therapist in evidence. Erasures or pencil notes are an indication of a problem to the claims reviewer, although initialled, clearly crossed out and corrected errors are quite legitimate.[4]

All records generated by the therapist, including initial, progress, and discharge reports should be signed by the appropriate person and dated (month, day, and year). When documentation is accomplished by assistants or students, the full name of the assistant and title (for example, S.P.T. for Student Physical Therapist) is used, and the document co-signed by the Registered or Licensed Physical Therapist (R.P.T. or L.P.T.) The physical therapist is responsible for the content of the record. The initial note should be recorded on the first day of treatment. It should contain the therapist's objective evaluation of the patient, including his diagnosis, the proposed treatment, and the location and severity of the injuries. Any pre-existing conditions should be mentioned. Minimum test results should include range of motion and muscular strength and assessment of function.

During the course of treatment, any changes in the referring doctor's orders, or the responses of the patient to therapy should be recorded. An assessment of the patient's mental attitude toward treatment is important in many cases. When the therapy involves equipment, exact positioning, calibrations, resistance or temperature settings, length of time, and numbers of repetitions should also be documented in the notes.

The final progress note should have been entered at the time of discharge, and should include a comparison of the patient's condition at discharge with that recorded at the time of the initial treatment. Any further recommendations, such as a home-treatment regimen or a future appointment should be noted.

"The patient's chart is a document with many uses," concludes Wessman. In order for it to serve these uses, it is subject to interpretation by many different people and should be written so that it is informative and easily understood by all.[5]

The Referral

In order to be considered for reimbursement by Medicare, a physical therapy program "must be directly and specifically related to an active treatment regimen designed by [a] physician." Even in states which allow direct access by the patient to the therapist, this principle will also apply to personal injury and workmen's compensation cases, since in most cases, the patient is initially seen by a physician. Evidence of referral would include signed orders from the physician, a diagnosis, and/or a request for evaluation. Orders for physical therapy from a physician should contain specific instructions as to the modalities or procedures to be used as well as its frequency and duration, and must be followed until a change of orders is received. If evaluation or treatment was requested, the physical therapist devises the treatment plan. In this case, the treatment, including modalities and/or procedures, frequency and duration, must appear on the therapist's signed and dated initial report. Personal injury and workmen's compensation cases in states which do allow direct access should reflect a very clear record of the therapist's initial examination. In these situations, the accuracy and detail of the initial report is crucial.[6]

The Initial Report

The initial report is a crucial element of physical therapy documentation. Objective data is essential in an initial report since it provides the only reliable measure of subsequent progress. The plan of treatment should outline specific procedures aimed at the correction of a specific deficit. The selection of exercises or modalities should reflect professional sophistication and their expected therapeutic value in the achievement of functional goals. The initial note should delineate the starting point, and establish the direction of the program.[7]

The initial report should include the diagnosis, the onset date, the age of the patient, the treatment diagnosis and the secondary diagnosis. If it is a readmission or a patient with a chronic condition, the initial report should explain the rationale for this specific program of treatment. It should state the prior level of function preceding the present onset. It should include relevant items of the patient's medical history and mental attitude, and objective measurements of ROM, strength, and functional problems. It should also identify goals, both for the therapist, and for the patient and/or the patient's family. It should include an assessment of the patient's rehabilitation potential, the expected duration of treatment, the treatment plan (modality, procedure, education, frequency, duration, etc.), the discharge plan, and the date and signature of the physical therapist and physician, if applicable.[8]

The effectiveness of a physical therapist's evaluation of a patient usually increases as the therapist gains experience. An ideal and very thorough evaluation could include patient information from as many as fifteen major areas:

1. Background information from patient's chart
2. General appearance
3. General observations
4 Mental Status
5. Respiratory function
6. Pain
7. Range of motion
8. Muscle function
9. Sensation
10. Cortical integration (perception)
11. Reflexes and/or reactions
12. Control of fine and gross movement
13. Posture analysis
14. Gait
15. Functional activities besides gait (e.g. stairs, ramps, wheelchair activities)[9]

Progress Notes

Physical therapists' progress notes have become increasingly important documents in the claims review process. More so than ever before, many companies now require the submission of progress notes as a matter of routine. In many cases, progress notes are the only way of determining what therapy was actually performed. Progress notes are key documents to the claims reviewer. Progress notes should ideally show at least the date, treatment(s) performed, and the patient's response and/or complaints. It is often the only way, when confronted with terse billing statements or treatment summaries, of cross-referencing to determine what actually happened in a clinic on a daily basis.

The lack of documentation is a common problem in physical therapy cases. The rule of thumb, in the claims review process as well as in the courts, is "If it wasn't written, it wasn't done." Daily progress notes are the physical therapist's primary and most import means of validating reimbursement claims, and it is perfectly legitimate for claims reviewers to examine them closely for discrepancies, inconsistencies, or other evidence of inappropriate billing or treatment. The lack of progress notes has often made the crucial difference in litigation. On one case, a physical therapist claimed to treat a patient three times per week for ten weeks. Her bill showed thirty sessions, but she was able to produce only ten progress notes. She claimed that the notes were summary notes, that is notes entered once per week rather than daily. Without daily progress notes, however, there was no way of verifying that the therapy was actually performed. The claim was subsequently denied.

Poor documentation is almost as great a problem as lack of documentation. Incomplete or sloppily entered progress notes do little to validate a therapist's claim. For example, a therapist's bill might state that a patient received four modalities, such as hot pack, electrical stimulation, traction, and ultrasound, on a given date. However, his or her progress notes for that date report only that a hot pack applied to the neck of the patient. Which is correct? This is the kind of glaring discrepancy in documentation that should immediately raise a red flag in the mind of a claims reviewer. Billing statements charging for treatments that are not verified by progress notes should be considered invalid until proven otherwise.

Progress notes should be entered on each patient visit, and whenever changes occur. A summary report should be generated no less than once every two weeks. Progress notes should summarize changes in status: pain, ROM, motor control, function, ability to follow or retain instruction, and attitude. Progress toward goals should be assessed, with readjustments of goals or accomplishments noted. A discussion of the treatment plan or "action accomplished" should be included, including modalities and procedures, education, equipment ordered, or the need for evaluation or conference with others or a discharge plan.[10]

Progress notes should contain goal changes, treatment changes and/or discontinued treatments, observed changes in the patient's condition or attitude toward treatment, and appliances ordered. Ideally, a daily calendar should be maintained with each patient's chart to display the dates on which treatment was rendered. Progress notes should support the number of treatments indicated in the daily calendar.

One of the worst examples of poor documentation with progress notes is the "ditto note." For example, a therapist notes that in a particular session a patient received hot pack, ultra-sound, and electrical stimulation. Subsequent entries typically read "same as above," or "status quo," or "continued to follow treatment." The implication is that the patient received hot pack, ultra-sound, and electrical stimulation in each session, but one does not really know. The patient may have received only one or two modalities on some days, so the cost for the treatment should be less.

Daily recording of treatment, at a minimum, should document the treatment given, that is the modality, procedure, or activity, and the patient response, as measured in such aspects as change in weight-bearing status, amount of assistance required, distance ambulated, gait deviations, level of mobility, pain, spasm, change in functional status, etc., length of treatment time, and frequency.[11]

> *Commentary*
> *I have often said that physical therapists do not know when to discharge a patient.*
>
> *Nathaniel Randolph*

Discharge Reports

There are several points in a therapy program when treatment should be modified or discontinued. These include: when the patient has achieved the stated goals of the therapy; when no further improvement in the patient's condition can be expected; when the patient has "obtained maximum potential for medical improvement;" and when the condition has stabilized in cases of permanent disability. While the responsibility for modifying or discontinuing treatment is shared by the physical therapist and the attending physician, as a practical matter, in most cases the decision rests with the physical therapist.[12]

Continuation of therapy after functional goals have been achieved constitutes waste. Consider, for example, a typical worker's compensation case. Mr. Agnew suffered a legitimate shoulder injury. At the initial session, he had pain that caused a limitation of range of motion and function. After two weeks of treatment, his range of motion and function returned to normal, but he continued to complain of stiffness, achiness, and pain and treatment was continued on this basis. Mr. Agnew's complaints might have been alleviated just as well with aspirin or hot packs he could administer himself at home. This type of unnecessary care is called palliative or maintenance care.

Blindly following doctor's orders is another source of unnecessary care. The doctor in Mr. Agnew's case may have ordered therapy three times a week for four weeks. Even though normal function was restored after two weeks, and the patient should have been discharged, therapy was continued because it was ordered. The therapist in private practice had a financial incentive to draw out therapy to its fullest possible extent in this case.

Human nature is often a potent factor in the provision of palliative care. Mr. Agnew, to follow along with the previous example, may have proven to be a jolly, hail fellow well met, coming in three times a week, telling jokes, bringing cookies, a welcome respite from the office routine. Perhaps the staff looked forward to seeing him. When it came time to consider discharging a patient like Mr. Agnew, it may have been easier to remember his complaints of achiness or pain and decide to keep him on for another week or two.

Physicians are subject to similar pressures when ordering or certifying physical therapy. Physicians, particularly those in private practice, often develop long-term relationships with patients. A family doctor may find it difficult, out of feelings of friendship or loyalty, or merely out of the frustration of hearing the same compliant visit after visit, to deny therapy to a patient who complains of pain. Even though function may be normal, and medication could handle the chronic pain, a doctor may order several extra weeks of physical therapy to appease a special patient.

Discharge plans should include the amount of supervision required, the levels of patient/family education suggested, and the tentative discharge date. Discharge statements should contain a description of the patient's physical, functional, and mental status as compared to the initial report. They should also include a discharge program and indicate that it has been discussed with the recipient, that is patient, family member, or another facility. The recipient should be identified by name.

Billing Statements and Procedures

Physical therapists have traditionally billed by the ledger system. In this system, the therapist enters treatments provided to each patient each day. However, ledger entries are often very vague and generic. A typical ledger entry might read "one hour of physical therapy," which the therapist would then bill at his prevailing hourly rate. This system of ledger entries is similar to summary notes, and would be entirely satisfactory providing that complete progress notes were also kept to specify the services provided. However, as has been shown, adequate progress notes are relatively rare. In many cases there is no way to determine what services were actually performed. One might expect that one hour of physical therapy would be sufficient to encompass several modalities and/or procedures. On the other hand, the treatment may have been nothing more than the application of a hot pack.

In recent years, with the increasing computerization of medical records, Current Procedure Terminology [CPT] codes have been introduced in an effort to standardize and objectify the billing of medical services, including physical therapy. [See Appendix 3] Under the CPT coding system, each modality and procedure receives a unique code number. This would appear to be an improvement over the vague ledger method since the services provided by the physical therapist, instead of being lumped together as a generic entity, are identified and billed individually.

Paradoxically, the one advantage of the CPT system is also its most serious flaw. By billing for services individually, it encourages "unbundling" of physical therapy services. Services previously included in a generic "one hour of physical therapy," when broken out and charged individually, can generate three or four times the billable income in the same amount of time.

One recent case provides a graphic example of the way in which CPT coding can be used to inflate a bill. A patient was involved in an on-going cycle of therapy that involved three modalities, hot pack, electrical stimulation, and massage, to three separate areas, the neck, back, and knee. The physical therapist, using the ledger system, charged the patient one hour of physical therapy at the rate of forty-five dollars per hour for these services.

During this patient's treatment course, the physical therapist instituted a computerized billing system using the CPT format. His new system listed and charged each of the three modalities separately to each area at the rate of nineteen dollars each, for a total of $171 per treatment. From one session to the next, almost literally overnight, the therapist's bill to the same patient for the same services more than tripled. Merely by installing a computerized billing system, the therapist had, in effect, given himself an $126 per hour raise.

> *Commentary*
>
> *The current profession-wide practice of billing for individual treatments in physical therapy should be seriously reconsidered. Other professionals, lawyers, architects, and engineers, to name a few, charge for their time in evaluating a problem, not for the individual procedures or calculations involved. It would be ludicrous for the engineering profession, for example, to develop a fixed schedule of charges for the various equations involved in developing a structural analysis. Yet this is precisely what physical therapists have done in adopting unbundling their charges.*
>
> *Nathaniel Randolph*

EVALUATING CLAIM DOCUMENTATION

Generally, documentation submitted to medical insurance intermediaries should be objective, complete, reliable, and in conformance with established regulations. Documentation submitted with reimbursement requests should demonstrate that a patient's program of therapy was justified, and should be consistent with the bill.

The reviewer should consider it the therapist's responsibility to deliver a clear, accurate, and objective view of all aspects of patient care. The documentation provided should be complete, demonstrate the need for skilled services, and evidence sound clinical judgment.[13]

To optimize his time, it might be useful for a reviewer to make several passes through a claims documentation packet. The first pass would check to see that all materials are included, and that all technical requirements of his firm or agency have been met. The second pass might verify the logic of the documents, that is, that no obvious discrepancies, such as correct names and dates, exist. Often, a claim can be rejected, or at least returned for additional information, on the basis of a very brief and cursory examination. Only once the claim has withstood the initial inspection need one spend much time on more time-consuming analyses. For the sake of convenience, the following discussion has been reduced to an abbreviated checklist of questions which the claims reviewer may wish to use. Experienced reviewers will add to or modify the question list in keeping with the policy of their own organization and state, and add appropriate items. As a generic list, however, the questions apply in many situations.

22-POINT CLAIMS REVIEW CHECKLIST

All questions should be answered with a yes if the claim is to be approved; one or more "no" answers raise questions as to the legitimacy of the claim.

FIRST AND SECOND PASS:
COMPLETION

- ☐ 1. Are required agency or company-specific forms completed?
- ☐ 2. Are physician orders included and signed?
- ☐ 3. Is there a report of initial visit?
- ☐ 4. Is there a set of progress notes?
- ☐ 5. Is itemized billing statement included?

DISCREPANCIES

- ☐ 6. Is the level of care consistent with insurer's policy and/or usual and customary standards?
- ☐ 7. Is the date sequence logical? (Is there an absence of unexplained gaps in treatment?)
- ☐ 8. Is there consistency between billing statements and patient progress notes?
- ☐ 9. Is there consistency between weekly summaries and daily progress notes?
- ☐ 10. Is the number of visits consistent with the diagnosis?
- ☐ 11. Is the duration of treatment consistent with the treatment plan?
- ☐ 12. Is the frequency of visits appropriate?

THIRD AND FOURTH PASSES:

CAUSALITY

- ☐ 13. Was the area(s) treated consistent with the claimed injury and the initial diagnosis, emergency room report, or incident report?
- ☐ 14. Are the actual treatments consistent with the plan or order?
- ☐ 15. Is the follow-up consistent with the initial visit?
- ☐ 16. If there were several providers, are their diagnoses and findings consistent with each other?

ANALYSES:

- ☐ 16. Was the treatment reasonable and necessary or indicated by the findings?
- ☐ 17. Was skilled physical therapy care required?
- ☐ 18. Was treatment plan directed at functional restoration of the identified problems?
- ☐ 19. Did the therapist avoid duplicative, redundant, or palliative treatments?
- ☐ 20. Did the patient show significant improvement?
- ☐ 21. If improvement reached a plateau, was treatment modified or terminated?
- ☐ 22. Were the treatment goals met?

ITEMS TO BE REVIEWED AND CHECKED

Review for completeness

The reviewer should make sure that the claim includes complete records including orders, certification, initial report, daily treatment notes, progress notes, and itemized billing statements. He or she should then check to see that the technical requirements for claims of the organization have been met, and if the treatment involves a covered level of care.

Review for initials and signatures

All orders, certifications, and notes must be signed and dated. A rubber stamp as a substitute for a signature from a referring physician is unacceptable on orders or certifications. All progress notes, including those entered by aides must be signed and dated by the physical therapist.

Review for complete orders and notes

Verifying whether a claim is complete and correct can involve a straightforward checklist like that presented above, but the reviewer should be sure to adapt the checklist to his or her particular organization and state. Checking for completion is a logical first step. Claims lacking orders, or progress notes, for example, are unacceptable. It may be, especially if the claim emanates from a large hospital or clinic, that the medical records included in the claim were for the wrong billing period. Treatments should match orders and the dates should correspond logically, with no unexplained long gaps.

Review for billing statements and progress notes

The billing statements should correspond with the progress notes. Billing statements should contain the dates of service, the start of care date, the treatment diagnosis, the onset date for that diagnosis, and the number of visits and/or treatments provided. The diagnosis appearing on the bill may not match that for which the patient receives physical therapy, an indication of a serious problem. Such a discrepancy may well be a clerical error but, unless clarified, constitutes grounds for denial. One way of "unbundling" services is to charge each treatment modality separately for each area treated. Several modalities can ordinarily be administered to several areas in a single visit. If the number of modalities seems excessive, services may have been unbundled in this manner. The billings statements should be cross checked with the progress notes.

Review for date sequences

Merely checking dates can be a prime indicator of irregularities. It would take a remarkably prescient therapist to begin treating a condition before the injury has occurred. If the start of care date is reported on or before the onset date of the diagnosis, the reviewer has a real reason to doubt the honesty of the claim! A pre-existing injury or condition should be considered suspect.

Review for specificity of orders

Orders from the physician submitted with claims should be complete and specific. Phrases such as "treat PRN" (as needed) "modalities as needed" are not specific and are unacceptable. Orders for the duration and frequency of treatment should also be specific. For example, orders calling for treatment "two-three times/week for four-six weeks" are vague and open ended. Although it seems obvious, check to make sure that the treatment given matches the orders.

Review for discrepancies and inconsistencies

Discrepancies are the best clues to discover bill inflation or other fraudulent activities in physical therapy claims. It is important to review all the documentation involved in a claim, comparing particularly the initial evaluation reports of the physicians and therapists involved. When one compares dates and evaluations, discrepancies often become glaringly obvious. Sometimes, an accident victim who complained of only one or two problems in the emergency room after an accident will show up in a doctor's office several weeks later complaining of pain in several areas, and subsequently receive months of treatment. This pattern is very suspicious. Certainly, stiffness frequently appears the day following an accident. However, if the problems were serious enough to require months of therapy they should have shown up in the emergency room or within the first few days of the accident.

Sometimes the inconsistencies in documentation will be so pronounced that the same patient, as described in the initial evaluation reports of sequential doctors and therapists, will look like several different people. The report of doctor number one, the initially consulted physician or the attending emergency room physician, might note several different areas of injury. Then the patient is referred to a specialist, say a neurologist or an orthopedist, who treats only one or two areas. Of course a specialist, by definition, limits his treatment to specific areas or systems. However, he may note in his initial evaluation that the patient elicited no other complaints.

Occasionally even more obvious discrepancies will crop up in evaluation reports. Doctor number one may record severely limited range of motion, weakness, and/or severe tenderness and spasms, whereas doctor number two, examining the same patient within one or two days, will report none of these findings.

The reports of the physical therapist can often point out discrepancies in a claim. Comparison of doctor number one's evaluation with the therapist's notes might show that the patient actually received treatment only for one or two of the problem areas reported by the attending physician or vice versa.

Review for need for skilled physical therapy

The reviewer might initially scan for some obvious irregularities. Was there indeed a need for skilled therapy? Flags indicating the lack of need for skilled therapy include the performance of routine range of motion exercises, when the notes document normal range of motion.

Do the records indicate that the services were not directed to functional restoration but rather to palliative or maintenance care? This might be the case if there were long periods of repetitive service, insignificant improvement or a plateau in progress, an inability to sustain goals, or signs of no overall improvement. Many insurers, including Medicare, will not pay for maintenance care.

Does the care appear to be reasonable and necessary given the recorded diagnosis, problems, treatment plan, goals, and rehabilitation potential? Are there any indications of duplication of service among other physical therapists, nurses, technicians, or physicians, for example, the application of hot packs at the doctor's office in addition to the physical therapist's treatment?

The services provided should be sufficiently sophisticated or complex as to justify the participation of a licensed, trained physical therapist. If someone other than a physical therapist, or even the patient himself, could safely provide the care, then the services of a physical therapist may not be required. Unless complicated by an underlying condition, palliative modalities such as hot and cold packs, TENS, ambulation, and repetitive exercise, can often be accomplished without skilled supervision, subsequent to initial instruction. Furthermore, if the progress of a patient's medical condition indicates a likelihood of recovery to a former state of function without intervention, then therapy may not be medically necessary or reasonable. The services of the Physical Therapist may be required for only one treatment such as for instruction in a home exercise program, which may be all that is needed.

Review for progress towards goal

A program that continues unchanged for several months suggests that a high level of professional sophistication might not have been required or was absent. In cases of maintenance care, where a patient has already successfully completed a program of rehabilitation, the role of the physical therapist can safely be confined to evaluation and infrequent oversight. Maintenance programs he or she prescribes can safely be conducted by supportive technical staff, or by the patient at home. Such care may not be necessary or appropriate for the treatment of the insured event, particularly if the patient reached maximum medical improvement.

Medicare insists that goals for therapy be reasonable and achievable within a predictable period of time and insurers in other areas have a right to expect reasonable results. Medicare considers "reasonable" to mean that there is a greater than fifty percent probability that the patient will make significant functional improvement as a result of physical therapy. The frequency and duration of treatment specified is regarded as a knowledgeable estimate by the therapist of how long it will take the patient to achieve the expected goals. If it becomes clear at some point during treatment that goals will not be met, the continuation of physical therapy services can be considered no longer reasonable.

It should be remembered that the restoration of function is the primary aim of physical therapy. Therefore, an increase in range of motion, endurance, or strength alone should not be considered significant improvement unless these gains can be shown to translate directly to improvements in functional skills. Physical therapists must clearly and objectively document functional progress in order for therapy services to be considered reasonable. When no functional progress is evident over a period of time, therapy becomes palliative or "maintenance care." In the case of minor soft tissue injuries where there are only subjective complaints of pain or discomfort, if there is no funtional loss, then the treatment is obviously Palliative.

As the name implies, progress reports should demonstrate progress toward stated or established goals. They should contain objective data that can be compared to the initial report. Progress reports should provide reassessments of short and long term goals as dictated by the patient's condition. Lack of progress over a period of time is not necessarily an indicator of mal-utilization, but such cases require scrutiny. In these instances, the therapist should indicate that he has recognized the problem and reevaluated the patient, perhaps setting more conservative goals. Lack of progress always indicates the treatment program needs to be re-evaluated or that some other medical intervention may be indicated.

A well-conceived program of therapy will include educational components. It is important that the patient and the patient's family understand the aims and logic of the therapy. The home can become an ideal extension of the clinic especially as the patient's progress in therapy translates into functional gains in day-to-day activities. The nursing staff is an ideal conduit for educational modalities. Use of a clinical staff in this manner may display to the reviewer a well-balanced, team-oriented approach to the management of a patient's program.

Review for chronic conditions

Documentation should differentiate between acute and chronic conditions. In general, acute, or new, problems may require a longer duration of therapy than chronic, or older, problems. Documentation should establish prior levels of function and demonstrate clearly the need for physical therapy to achieve functional goals at that particular time. Patients suffering from chronic conditions such as Parkinson's disease or multiple sclerosis are likely to have a poor potential for rehabilitation, and have a less compelling need for intensive therapy.[14]

Review for palliative modalities

Prolonged use of modalities such as hot packs, infrared, ice packs, paraffin baths, and whirlpool should be regarded with skepticism unless they are shown to have been applied as an integral part of a larger rehabilitative program. By themselves, such modalities are useful in temporarily reducing pain, but unless the reduction of pain is required to engage in exercises or other therapy, it is only a palliative program. Since physical therapy is directed at restoration of function, such pain treatment, which may not require the services or the expense of a physical therapist, is often not appropriate to the insurance claim, beyond the first several weeks.

Review for unassisted exercise

Active range of motion exercises should also be regarded skeptically. Exercise which is billed for should be documented for its need or therapeutic value. Legitimate instances of therapist-assisted exercise would include cases where the patient cannot perform the exercises safely on his own, or where pain or another complication requires that the patient receive physical assistance in performing the prescribed exercise. A patient who performs active range of motion exercises or merely needs assistance in attaching an ankle weight for strength exercise, for example, probably does not require the attention of a highly- trained professional for his sessions and should be placed at a lower level of supervision.

Review for plateaus in treatment

The claims reviewer should be alert for plateaus where treatment seems to have become merely routine or palliative. This might be indicated if the patient does not seem to progress for several weeks. For example, the patient performs only active range of motion exercises without progressive resistance or weights and the evaluation indicated that the patient had normal range of motion and/or strength.

Modalities such as hot packs, cold packs, and TENS, for example, have been proven to be safe and effective treatments that can be performed by the patient himself at his home. The clinical setting is not necessary for these treatments alone. A record indicating only those codes, in the absence of other aspects of a treatment program, is clearly suspect. In this fashion, a reviewer confronted with a CPT-coded account can sometimes quickly identify claims without merit. For example, by consulting Appendix 3, it would be quite clear that a claim for categories 97010 (hot packs) only, was not appropriate, whereas one showing that modalities coupled with 97110 (therapeutic exercise) would make more sense. See Appendix 3 for a complete listing of modality codes used in physical therapy.

A FINAL WORD

All treatments and services that are billed must be documented. On all passes through clinical documentation, follow the rule "If it wasn't written it wasn't done."

CHAPTER FOUR ENDNOTES

1. General Accounting Office, "Medicare Rehabilitation Service Claims Paid Without Adequate Information" (GAO/HRD 87-91), (Washington, D.C., 1987), as quoted in Carole Bernstein Lewis, *Documentation: The PT's Course on Successful Reimbursement*, (Bethesda, MD. :Professional Health Educators, Inc., 1987), p.3.
2. John Echternach, "Use of the Problem-Oriented Clinical Note in a Physical Therapy Department," *Physical Therapy* 54 (January 1974): pp. 19-22.
3. Henry C. Wessman, "Progress Notes," *Journal of the American Physical Therapy Association*, n.d., reprinted in American Physical Therapy Association, *Progress Notes for Physical Therapy* [PNPT] (Alexandria, VA., n.d.): p. 3.
4. Ibid., p. 2.
5. Ibid., p. 3.
6. *Outpatient Physical Therapy Provider Manual* (HIM 9, Section 205.5,) as quoted in Lauren Hebert, "Basics of Medicare Documentation for Physical Therapy"), *Clinical Management 1* (January/February 1981): p. 13.
7. Hebert, p. 19.
8. Bernstein, p. 28.
9. Isabelle Bohman and D. Lavonne Jaeger, "Guidelines for Patient Evaluation," *Physical Therapy* 53 (October 1973), reprinted in PNPT, p. 14.
10. Bernstein, p. 29.
11. Ibid.
12. State of Washington Department of Labor and Industries, Industrial Insurance Division, "Provider Bulletin," Olympia, WA., 1990., p. 3.
13. Bernstein, p. 29.
14. Ibid., p. 30.

5

The Claims Review Process

Claims Review in Cost-Containment
Screening to Determine Reviewable Cases
Simplified or Generic Case Flow
Checklist of Screening Criteria
Liaison Between Screener abd PT Reviewer
PT Claims Review: The Logic of the Process
Documentation Checklist
Some Basics
"SOAP" as a Key
The Common-Sense Expert

CLAIMS REVIEW IN COST-CONTAINMENT

As the cost of medical claims and the consequent cost of insurance climbed over the 1980s, the public, state legislatures, and insurance companies sought means to control costs. Insurance firms tried a varied of cost-containment systems. As we have seen, identifying and rejecting unnecessary or unethical claims for physical therapy could greatly reduce insurance claims, and would assist in holding down the costs to the public in the form of caps on premiums. But how should the abusive, fraudulent, or incorrect claims be identified, and on what logic should they be rejected?

Insurance adjusters might suspect that treatment was inappropriate, but rejecting a claim on their own suspicion alone would not stand up under a legal attack in court. The claimant's attorney would simply be able to ask the adjuster: "Where did you get your medical training? Are you a licensed physical therapist?" Thus, the effective pursuit of cost containment through rejecting excessive or unnecessary claims had to result from a joint effort between professionals with different kinds of backgrounds. This chapter is intended to show to the professional insurance claims specialist how to work with consulting claims reviewers who are themselves physical therapy specialists. By understanding the claims review process, as it should be ideally carried out, the insurance professional can seek out and find the most effective claims review personnel and firms outside of the company and use their expertise to identify and deny inappropriate or excessive claims. Between 1983 and 1989, the number of utilization review firms in the United States climbed rapidly from zero to about 200. As insurance companies evaluated the quality of the consulting services, the intense competition among review firms began to produce a "shake out" of those firms, with consolidation and absorption of smaller companies, the *Wall Street Journal* reported in late 1989. As insurers sought higher-quality review, standards and expectations rose.[1]

There are no **formal** standards for physical therapy reviewers, but the APTA encourages the practice of review by Registered Physical Therapists who are actively engaged in physical therapy practice themselves. The reasoning is that reviewers who maintain a practice will remain in touch with the changing technology, and that reviewers who derive all of their income from review rather than practice might have an inappropriate incentive to increase their recommendations for denial. The APTA holds that a reviewer may not ethically enter an arrangement in which payment is linked to the number of recommendations to deny claims.[2]

Actual denial of claims can only be carried out by a licensed claims adjuster in most jurisdictions. Yet the adjuster does not ordinarily have training in physical therapy or in allied medical fields. Thus, the adjuster must obtain an independent review when a claim is suspect. If the independent reviewer is able to identify problems in a file, and is willing and able to testify in court as to the reasoning process which led him to report that there were problems about the reasonableness or necessity of the care in a particular case (what is called a "Negative Finding"), then the cooperative structure is working.

However, to be efficient, the insurance professional should send to the reviewer only those cases which appear to have serious problems. For these reasons, the insurance professional should have some understanding of the logic and approach of the good reviewer, and should send cases which have internal evidence of a problem.

SCREENING TO DETERMINE REVIEWABLE CASES

At first, when submitting cases to outside review or to utilization review consultants, insurance companies proceeded with little or no system of identifying potentially rejectable cases. Instead, they would simply pick out the most complicated, most expensive, or even the "thickest files" for outside review. However, as insurance firms sought effective cost-containment methods, a number of more sophisticated and systematic ways of identifying those cases most likely to benefit from outside utilization review developed. This process of identifying, at the company, those cases which should be forwarded for outside professional review is differently organized and differently named from company to company. For purposes of discussion in this work we will refer to the process as "Case Screening."

In one company, Case Screening will be conducted by the Claims Adjuster; in another, the person doing the screening will be an "Expediter," a "Claims Examiner," or a "Claims Specialist." In some firms, Telephone Adjusters, in minor cases with low coverages, can investigate cases by telephone and resolve them quickly. In those firms, cases which have higher coverages are routed to Adjusters, who perform the screening function, deciding which cases need to be submitted for outside review. In those cases which have problems with the physician side of the claim, the Screener (however designated) may refer the case to an in-house specialist. The internal specialists may have training as nurses and the company may designate them as "Medical Coordinators." Medical Coordinators serve in an intermediary level between the initial Screeners and outside Reviewers, deciding some cases and referring others back to the Adjuster with the recommendation for outside utilization review. Physicians employed by insurance firms in such an intermediate role are often referred to as "Medical Directors."

Parts of the screening process can be reduced to statistics and performed by computer programs which incorporate expert knowledge to identify cases which have the appearance of an irregularity. Some insurance companies have incorporated computerized screening in order to identify the cases for review either internally or by outside reviewers.

Many sorts of irregularities are caught at the stage of Screening, or by the in-house medical personnel. For example, unnecessary diagnostic testing which is unrelated to the nature of the injury can be spotted and a denial recommended. Several such irregularities would suggest that the case should be reviewed in its entirety. The abuse of diagnostic testing, either through over-charging for particular tests, or through the administering of un-needed or irrelevant tests is a major contributor to spiralling health-care costs. Some computer-based systems of screening particularly focus on irrelevant or excessive testing, and flag such cases for review. Metropolitan Life Insurance installed such a system in 1986 and calculated that it saved between $4 and $5 for every dollar expended on the system.[3]

There is considerable variation from company to company in the way in which cases are screened and the way in which decisions are reached to seek outside utilization review. The table presented here represents, in a generic fashion, the flow process of a claim from processing to adjuster.

Simplified or Generic Case Flow

Cases referred outside for review by a specialist in physical therapy, usually a Registered Physical Therapist or a consulting firm through which RPTs work, are the special subject of this chapter. Most insurance firms would designate the person doing this task as a "Physical Therapy Claims Reviewer." As there is considerable variation in terminology, structure, and organization, in this chapter we will designate as "Screener" (with a capital "S") the person at the insurance firm making the decision whether or not to seek outside review, whether that person is titled as Adjuster, Claims Expediter, or has some other title. Similarly, we will designate as "PT Reviewer" (with a capital "R") the person conducting physical therapy claims review in a consulting capacity, whether that person works individually or through a utilization review organization.

The Screener, who works with particular PT Reviewers, in addition to using established guidelines, usually will develop an intuitive sense of exactly what sorts of cases are reasonable and beneficial to send for outside review. Screeners who need to decide whether a case is appropriate for further review should be familiar with the approaches adopted by PT Reviewers. Experience will teach that certain cases are more likely to receive a Negative Finding or a report of lack of reasonable or necessary care than others. Clearly, it is more cost-effective to send more of those cases which are likely to yield a Negative Finding, than to simply include a great variety of legitimate claims which would represent a waste of the time and the consulting fees of the Physical Therapy Claims Reviewers. Hence, some Screeners have developed Checklists, or Identifying Flags. Some insurers have developed, leased, or purchased computer-based systems of screening which identify through statistics the cases most likely to receive a Negative Finding and which will be most profitably submitted to an outside utilization review consultant. Other insurance firms turn all cases above a certain dollar amount over to a UR firm, which does its own computer screening and then submits particularly outstanding cases to its own group of consultants for outside review.

However organized, the most efficient Screening should incorporate some systematic approach, based on the company's own experience. However, certain elements are commonly and logically included in the Screener's Checklist of Screening Criteria or List of Identifying Flags of Abuse.

THE ACCIDENT GAME

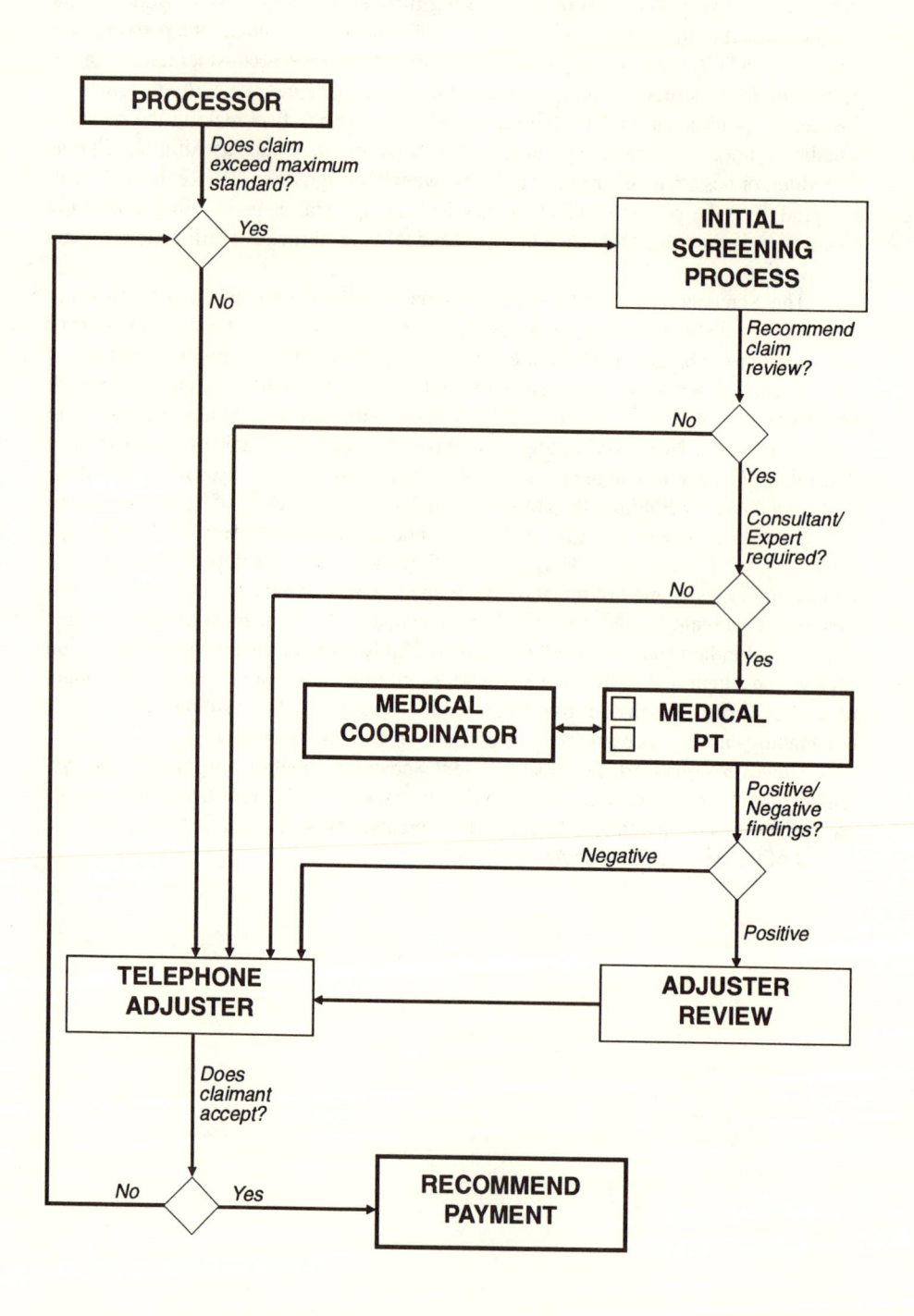

```
PROCESSOR
   │
   │ Does claim exceed maximum standard?
   ▼
   ◇ ── Yes ──▶ INITIAL SCREENING PROCESS
   │                      │
   No                     │ Recommend claim review?
   │                      ▼
   │              No ──◇── Yes
   │                      │
   │                      │ Consultant/Expert required?
   │                      ▼
   │              No ──◇── Yes
   │                      │
   │                      ▼
   │           MEDICAL COORDINATOR ◀──▶ MEDICAL PT
   │                                        │
   │                                        │ Positive/Negative findings?
   │                                        ▼
   │                          Negative ──◇── Positive
   │                                        │
   ▼                                        ▼
TELEPHONE ADJUSTER ◀──────────────── ADJUSTER REVIEW
   │
   │ Does claimant accept?
   ▼
 No ──◇── Yes ──▶ RECOMMEND PAYMENT
```

CHECKLIST OF SCREENING CRITERIA

☐ Excessive dollar amount [over: $_____]

☐ Excessive duration of treatment [longer than:____ weeks]

☐ Excessive frequency of treatment [more than __ times/week]

☐ Excessive total number of treatments (over 20 or 30)

☐ Excessive diagnostic testing

☐ Diagnostic testing unrelated to treated problem

☐ Duplication of diagnostic testing

☐ Palliative (hot pack) only

☐ Time gap between causal incident and seeking initial care

☐ Time gaps in care

☐ Evidence of attorney-directed care

(Firm-Specific Criteria:)

_____

_____

_____

[Copyright to this page is waived and contents are to be regarded as in the public domain. Photocopying permitted.]

The insurance Screener should set specific parameters for each of these categories in discussion with the PT Reviewer, based on the firm's policy, its experience, and variations in state law and practice. Firms operating in states with caps on no-fault claims, for example, would adjust the dollar amounts to those caps. Experience and the accumulation of Negative Findings in certain types of cases by PT Reviewers can readily lead to the expansion of the CHECKLIST OF SCREENING CRITERIA. For these reasons, the specific numbers in certain criteria are left blank and space is provided for the addition of firm-specific criteria. The sheet may be photocopied and utilized, with the appropriate adaptations.

LIAISON BETWEEN SCREENER AND PT REVIEWER

After cases have been selected by the Screener and sent to the Physical Therapy Claims Reviewer, ideally, the Claims Reviewer will follow a specific and logical process in identifying those cases which demonstrate a problem with the reasonableness or necessity of the indicated care. The logic of the thought process and the proper writing format for the review is provided here so that the insurance professional acting in the role of Screener, in setting policy, or in a position to evaluate and select outside PT Reviewers, will be able to understand the sorts of thinking brought to bear by the PT Reviewer. But even more importantly, if the Screener understands the logic employed by the PT Reviewer, the liaison between the two will be more effective.

If the Adjuster or Screener is aware of the thought process used by a senior PT Reviewer, some of the same logic can be applied at the early stage when cases are referred outside for review. If the Screener has identified a number of specific problems in a file, and asks the outside PT Reviewer to apply professional experience to evaluating those possible problems and discrepancies, then the work of the PT Reviewer will be made somewhat easier. For such reasons, a good and detailed understanding of the logic and thought process of a senior PT Reviewer is extremely useful to those doing the Screening and referral. Questions, problems, discrepancies, gaps and other irregularities can be noted by the Screener and brought to the PT Reviewer's attention. As a non-medical professional, the Screener may or may not have identified a real problem; however, if some element of the case strikes the Screener as improper, it should be noted for attention by the PT Reviewer.

In a system in which Screening is an automatic or statistical process, the "Screens" or "Edits" which single out problem cases will be explicit. In systems in which Screening is done more subjectively, and particularly where a specific Screener or Claims Adjuster has developed a working relationship with a specific PT Reviewer, the communication of particular reasons for identifying a problem file can make the liaison even more effective. The sophisticated Screener, by identifying the areas with problems and by asking questions, provides focus to the PT Reviewer, who can then bring the judgment of a professional physical therapist to bear.

PT CLAIMS REVIEW: THE LOGIC OF THE PROCESS

Those PT Reviewers providing high-quality review of claims will proceed along the lines suggested here, and will be able to apply their own knowledge of the nature of professional physical therapy practice to evaluate whether or not a particular claim should receive Negative Findings.

Step one: Check for completeness

The physical therapist acting as a PT Reviewer needs to be certain that the case examined is complete. Thus the PT Reviewer will make a pass through the case documents provided to guarantee, not only that the documentation in the physical therapy section of the case meets the standards as detailed in Chapter Four, but that the whole case is completely documented. A draft checklist is included here, but the PT Reviewer will need to modify the list provided to fit special state features and any firm-specific requirements.

DOCUMENTATION CHECKLIST

☐ Report of Circumstances of the Injury:
  in auto: Police Accident Reports;
  in Workmen's Compensation: OTJ Accident Report,
  usually filed by Risk Assessment Officer or the employer's Safety Officer

☐ Emergency Room Report [or]

☐ Report of initial attending physician

☐ Reports from any other consulting physicians
  office notes
  diagnostic tests
  treatment plans

☐ Physical Therapy records:
☐ Physical Therapy prescription
☐ Initial visit report
☐ Assessments
☐ Progress reports
☐ Diagnostic testing results
☐ Subsequent testing results
☐ Daily progress notes
☐ Billing statements
☐ Firm-specific forms:

_____
_____
_____

Copyright to this page is waived. It may be photocopied for use.

In addition, Workmen's Compensation cases may also include reports from Vocational Rehabilitation Counselors, and may include a report from a Case Manager. In these cases, a "Discharge Report," which certifies that the employee was capable of returning to work may also be included. In other compensation cases there may be a Disability Report, showing the degree of temporary or permanent impairment of function.

Some PT Reviewers prefer to make several passes through a claims documentation packet, taking notes, before beginning the Narrative. In this process, the first pass would be to check for completeness. Again, a personally-created or personally-modified checklist would be most useful at this point, depending on policy, coverage, and the sort of cases being reviewed.

Step two: Discrepancy check

A later pass requires a look at the logical sequence of the documents, to spot obvious discrepancies in names, dates and treatments. Some such discrepancies may have been observed by the Screener, noted, and included in the correspondence transmitting the case for review.

Step three: Reading and analysis

On assuring that the case is complete, the PT Reviewer will read the whole case. The PT Reviewer will develop a written Case Narrative or "sequence of events" while reading the case, specifying, by date, when the patient was injured, when and under what conditions the patient sought treatment, and noting the referrals for treatment. As the Narrative is developed, the PT Reviewer may simply dictate the comments into a recorder and have them later typed for editing, or the PT Reviewer may work directly into a word-processor. Some PT Reviewers write out their Narrative as notes, then put the notes through a draft and editing stage. The actual writing process varies with personal work habits. However, there should be a Case Narrative authored by the PT Reviewer. Some may prefer to call it a Sequence of Events, or a Chronological Account.

An analytic and perceptive thought-process in constructing the Narrative is essential to good review. That thought process uses the "SOAP" principle, as developed by Dr. Weed and described earlier in this text, to evaluate each contact between the patient and various health professionals. What were the Subjective complaints of the patient? What were the Objective findings of diagnostic testing? How did the physician or physical therapist diagnose, evaluate, or "Assess" the patient? What Plan or treatment system did the physician or physical therapist suggest? Applying these "SOAP" questions to the reports, the Reviewer looks for causal relationships, discrepancies, and whether treatment resulted in significant changes in patient's condition. Was the treatment used appropriate for the injury? Did the treatment meet the stated or obvious goals? The same question of logical connection between findings, assessment, and treatment plan or modifications of treatment, will be applied to each of the several physicians, therapists, and consultants contacted by the patient. All follow-up evaluations, even though they would normally be more brief than the initial visits, would be subjected to the same set of questions.

While reading over the reports, the PT Reviewer asks, "Is all this indicated, based on the diagnosis and the injury that was described?"

Many physical therapists will actually format their progress notes with marginal indications of "S" "O" "A" and "P," in order to remind themselves to enter a remark under subjective, objective, assessment, and plan. Even in such cases, however, some therapists fail to document any objective finding to support the patient's complaint, or upon which to base an assessment. Despite the reminder, many therapists simply note the patient's complaints and describe the treatment delivered and recommended. In such a situation, the records neither validate nor objectively substantiate the claimed impairment of function in the assessment, nor do they support the need for the care recommended in the treatment plan.

> *Commentary*
> *People with sloppy documentation get burned.*
> *Nathaniel Randolph*

One constant question in the PT Reviewer's mind, reflected in the Narrative, is whether or not the complaints and treatments were causally related to the incident for which the insurance is claimed. Did the treatment meet the stated goals or was it palliative? Was it appropriate to the injuries. The symptoms that are being reported, whether subjectively or objectively, should be caused by the accident. If the emergency room said that Mrs. Baker hurt her knee, why is she complaining of pain in her shoulder, or her back? True, people tighten up the next day or a few days later, but then the question arises, why was there no early report? It is still something to keep in mind, especially in a case, for example, in which the patient required lots of therapy and treatment to the back, but had never complained about the back over the first few weeks of treatment. The backache may have been real, but it did not derive from the accident, if a long period went by without complaint after the accident. The Reviewer should question if back symptoms were a result of the accident since it was not initially documented.

The PT Reviewer's Narrative will support the Findings. As the PT Reviewer proceeds chronologically through the story of the case, the report should show the reader discrepancies, gaps, inappropriate treatments, questionable care, duplicative modalities, or other irregularities. If there were such problems, and they are noted in the Narrative, the story will emerge, and a summary of the discrepancies or gaps will support the final Finding. In the chronological summary or Narrative of the case, the discrepancies are revealed as one reads along; the evidence will be there which forms part of the argument at the Finding. In passing, the Narrative might note, "On such and such a date, Dr. X indicated there was a limitation of ten degrees to range of motion. However, on that same date, Dr. Y noted there was normal range of motion."

A simple principle to apply in looking for discrepancies is to constantly use a Comparison of Findings--comparing diagnoses, comparing objective measurements, if any, comparing subjective comments.

Step four: Narrative or Sequence of Events

The analytic pass through the documents is used to develop the Narrative. The PT Reviewer asks a whole series of analytic questions: Is the date sequence logical? Are there unexplained gaps in treatment? Is the assessment substantiated by a logical agreement between the subjective and objective findings? Is the billing statement inconsistent with the patient progress notes? Are there any discrepancies between reevaluations and daily progress notes? Is the number of visits inconsistent with the treatment plan or orders? Is the duration of treatment inconsistent with the treatment plan? Is the frequency of visits inappropriate? Are the treatments inconsistent with the plan or order? Could the patient have performed the care at home or was professional care really required? Was the treatment plan sound in that it was directed at functional restoration or was it simply palliative? Was there evidence of duplicative or redundant treatment?

In particular, when looking at follow-up treatments, the PT Reviewer should be looking for change or lack of change. Was there a modification of the treatment in response to changed symptoms? If improvement reached a plateau, did the therapist modify or end the treatment? Again, "Comparison of Facts and Findings" is the approach. In some cases, the different follow- up visits to different consulting physicians may result in some very different descriptions; the file may seem as if it describes two or three different patients. The experienced PT Reviewer will develop a picture of the patient from the record; as the PT Reviewer then holds up to the scrutiny of Comparison of Facts and Findings later elements of the records, the image of a different patient with different conditions may begin to emerge. A discrepancy in objective tests and measurements is most revealing, for objective tests are supposed to be scientific, accurate, repeatable and should be relatively comparable between different providers. If the so-called objective results vary significantly, particularly on the same date, it is clear that a problem has been identified.

As the consulting physician reports and PT notes are reviewed, the PT Reviewer looks for every kind of discrepancy. Discrepancies in findings, discrepancies in areas of the body affected or treated, discrepancies in the indicated severity of the injury -- any of these would indicate a problem.

In workmen's compensation cases, the PT Reviewer would look at the Discharge Report, and ask, were the Goals of the therapy met? Did the Patient get better? Were there recommendations for further rehabilitation, "work-hardening", further training? Was the patient discharged as "fit for duty?" In workmen's compensation, the process is regulated by state statute, providing documents which certify that a patient is capable of working, or has a disability. In some instances, a "Case Manager" is called in by the insurance firm; the Case Manager is often a nurse, working in an overseeing role to bring the case to resolution, assuring that the case move along, and that the patient makes required appointments. In such cases, Case Manager notes and reports are similarly reviewed.

Other workmen's compensation and disability cases may include reports from a variety of specialists, each of which should be reviewed with an eye out for discrepancies: Claims Analysts, Claims Mangers, Disability Adjudicators, Rehabilitation Consultant, Rehabilitation Counsellors, and Occupational Nurse Consultants. Some cases will have psychiatric reports as well.

In personal bodily injury cases, the PT Reviewer should examine whether, at final discharge, there were any residual effects which could come back as recurrent problems, and should note any permanent or partial disabilities. Since state statutes require a Discharge Report of some sort before a workmen's compensation accident victim can return to work, such cases frequently have a more defined ending with a more clear-cut off point chronologically than personal bodily injury cases, in which the patient sometimes simply stops attending treatments.

Step five: Findings and Conclusions

The experienced PT Reviewer therefore keeps a wide variety of questions in mind during the development of the Narrative or Sequence of Events as the writing goes forward, indicating any noted discrepancies or apparent indications of inappropriate treatment. Thus, as the Narrative or Sequence of Events section is completed, and the PT Reviewer moves to writing Findings, a simple summary and restatement of discrepancies or questionable points already alluded to, serves to substantiate the argument at the end for a Negative Finding, if one is justified.

On the other hand, if the case appeared to be legitimate, and the care seemed reasonable and necessary, apparent discrepancies should be addressed and explained. Such a case could arise if a physician diagnosed a patient as having "shoulder pain," or possibly arthritis. In the same case, the physical therapist might assess that a frozen shoulder resulted and provide treatment for that condition. In effect, the physician's diagnosis was superceded by the more precise and accurate assessment of the physical therapist. In such cases, apparent discrepancies could arise, in the judgment of the PT Reviewer, which would be simple cases of different legitimate or honest interpretations of the same symptoms, and the PT Reviewer might very well send a Positive Finding to the Adjuster, if the care seemed reasonable. Such a case would be properly flagged and caught by the Screener, but the health care professional would judge the treatment as quite legitimate.

When the PT Reviewer reaches a Negative Finding, there should be a clear statement in the recommendation as to what section of the care seemed reasonable and necessary, and that section which the PT Reviewer found unreasonable. Often the division between proper and improper care is a matter of timing. Thus the PT Reviewer might find that all treatments up to the point of "Maximum Benefit" were reasonable and necessary, at a certain date. After that date, the progress notes might reveal only subjective complaints of pain, stiffness or soreness. But there might be either no record of Objective findings, such as tests indicating a restricted range of motion, or such tests, if taken, might indicate that the patient had reached maximum benefit as of a particular date. With reference to the date, the PT Reviewer should indicate, for example, "all treatment appeared reasonable and necessary until [date] when maximum benefit was achieved; after that date, the patient showed only minor complaints of pain, and therapy did not yield improvement in objective conditions." The PT Reviewer should always base Findings on specific information in the documentation--either specific information which was provided, or specific information, which by its absence, supported the Findings.

The key definition of physical therapy to keep in mind during the utilization review process is this: **The goal of physical therapy is the restoration of function**. Treatment which does not aim towards that goal is not reasonable and necessary. Thus, treatment which is simply palliative, or which extends beyond the point of maximum benefit is simply not justified. The PT Reviewer can "question" why the treatment continued beyond the point of Maximum Benefit. Palliative care represents an unnecessary expenditure of time and money and the insurance company should not be obliged to pay for unreasonable or unnecessary expenditures.

The PT Reviewer should recommend a level of reimbursement by noting the period of care which appeared reasonable and necessary, and those treatments which were appropriate. If the patient appeared to be fully recovered, the PT Reviewer might recommend referral to an Independent Medical Examiner (IME) for examination and evaluation to help substantiate the degree of recovery or to recommend further medical intervention.

Step six: Editing; checking the Review

Experienced PT Reviewers will find that their first drafts of the review need less editorial revision and correction than those written by PT Reviewers with less experience. However, no matter what level of experience, the review should be checked for several points. The following points are not to be considered "headings" in the review. Rather, they are checkpoints or editorial considerations that the PT Reviewer should use to insure that the review is professional. The insurance Adjuster can examine consultants' reviews with these considerations in mind to determine which of the consultants is providing the best quality reviews. Of course, the review should be professionally typed or word-processed, and should be free of typographical, spelling, or grammatical errors. It should be kept in mind that a physical therapy utilization review report very often becomes a legal document, part of the evidence material presented in court.

Sequence. The Narrative section of the review should tell the story of the injury and the treatment in correct chronological sequence through time, with internal reference to the key documentation which substantiates the story.

Discrepancies. The Narrative should include reference to contradictions and discrepancies internal to the visit to the PT, and any discrepancies between the PT's documentation and that of any examining physicians, neurosurgeons, physiatrists, orthopedists, or dentists. The documents should be referenced by issuing health care professional and by date so that the Adjuster or an attorney can readily identify them in the file. Discrepancies between PT reports and reports by any of the variety of disability or rehabilitation counsellors and consultants would be similarly identified and cited to the pertinent document.

Subjective and Objective symptoms. Objective results of examinations should be specifically noted, and the progress in alleviating those symptoms should be commented upon. Again, these comments should be linked to specific dates and documents in the file.

Relationship of Assessment and Plan to symptoms. The logic or lack of logic in the relationship between the planned and delivered therapy and the reported and measured symptoms should be commented upon.

Discrepancies in billing. Any particular double, triple, or even quadruple billing or redundancy in modalities should receive comment, as should any billed modalities not documented in the progress notes.

Point of Maximum Benefit. If the treatment was reasonable and necessary up to a particular point in time, but was excessive or unnecessary after that point, the review should allude to the specific documents which substantiate that point. By comparing the doctor's notes and the PT's notes, the PT Reviewer should be able to find the point, within those notes, where the benefits were at maximum, where the objective findings have returned to normal, or nearly normal, and where there are minimal or no subjective complaints. Merely complaining of soreness is no reason to be continuing physical therapy.

Findings. The PT Reviewer is not licensed to deny a claim or even to recommend its denial. Payment or denial of a claim is the responsibility of the Adjuster. Rather, the health-care professional is in the position of offering professional judgment on the reasonableness and necessity of care provided. In effect, the outside consultant is serving in the role of a utilization- reviewer, giving a retrospective professional assessment of the propriety of the care-utilization. Thus the findings should speak to that issue. If the care did indeed seem appropriate, and the billing accurate, the Positive Findings should be such that whatever problem alerted the initial Screener at the insurance firm is addressed and explained. If, on the other hand, in the judgment of the PT Reviewer, the care did not appear appropriate, the Negative Finding **must be substantiated by the record.**

Some Basics:

Conclusions rooted in Documents

It is not enough for PT Reviewers to say that in their professional judgment the care in particular cases was excessive. Such a line of argument would readily collapse in a court setting, simply because the nature of professional judgment is that it can vary from one professional to another. Rather, the PT Reviewer should base the Findings, not on general or abstract principles such as a general notion that a certain therapy should not exceed a certain number of visits, or a certain frequency of visits. This particular case, the patient's attorney could readily argue, may have required longer or more frequent treatment in the judgment of the billing PT. Similarly, the PT Reviewers should not simply indicate that for particular symptoms they would have recommended a different modality for the delivery of heat, for example. Again, variations on such points are well within the purview of professional judgment. For this reason, it is essential that the Findings not be based on the individual PT Reviewer's standard alone, but should be rooted in the particular documentation of the case at hand.

Commentary

The reason to tie your narrative to the documentation is that eventually you are going to go to court. Senior PT Reviewers only get those cases that are going to go into litigation anyway; they don't have to do the routine cases. The insurer knows the attorney for the patient is going to sue, or suit has already been filed, so you have to have your documents in line.

Nathaniel Randolph

"SOAP" AS A KEY

If a modality was not appropriate, the comment should indicate that there was no evidence of an objective finding which showed that it was necessary to deliver that particular modality. In effect, the S-O-A-P principle, as a reasoning process, provides the key to deciding on whether or not treatment was reasonable or necessary. **Subjective** complaints, linked with **objective** findings, properly **assessed**, produce a logical conclusion as to appropriate **plan** of treatment. If there was no objective finding, or if the assessment did not logically flow from that objective finding, the logical sequence which leads to reasonable and necessary care has been broken. A break in that sequence, if reflected in the documents, from the PT Reviewer's perspective, is evidence that the care may not have been reasonable or necessary. Unexplained contradictions in Objective findings also raise questions as to the reasonableness and necessity of care. Such points provide the proper focus, and such evidence should be the basis of a Negative Finding.

THE COMMON-SENSE EXPERT

Thus, if a Physical Therapy Claims Reviewer is called upon in expert testimony to defend the interpretation of a case in the report and to defend a Negative Finding, the logic used will be able to withstand close questioning. If the documentation provided with the case is the focal point, then the testifying PT Reviewer can deflect questions away from the question of variations in professional judgment, to a close review of the record provided with the case. If the documentation did not show objective findings, or if the objective findings noted as the result of diagnostic testing did not support an assessment, or if an assessment, as diagnosed, did not logically support a treatment, or if the documents revealed a purely palliative treatment, the testifying expert witness can direct the court's attention to those facts.

The logic in such situations is direct and clear, and it should be presented in a direct and clear fashion, so as to be convincing to judges, attorneys, and to a jury of lay persons. Since the logical principles are those of common sense, they can be presented in a very straightforward fashion. "There were no objective findings reflected in the documents to justify continuation of treatment beyond March 1st." The statement is clear and not at all confusing to a jury; it cannot be contradicted because it is based on an absence of evidence in the documented file. The file is in evidence. Everyone will understand that the treatment was not justified as necessary if there is no supporting objective indication of the need for the treatment.

If the court is reminded that the purpose of physical therapy is to restore function, and if it can be demonstrated, **from the record provided**, that some or all of the billed activity did not have that function, then the court, including a jury of laypersons, can be convinced that the claim was inappropriate.

On the contrary, a claims review which simply suggests a Negative Finding, because in the professional judgment of the PT Reviewer, a treatment seemed unnecessary or unreasonable, is far less useful to the Adjuster or to the attorney representing the case. If physical therapy is simply described as a variety of modalities which in the judgment of a therapist ought to be employed, then the plaintiff's attorney can suggest that the choice of modality and its application was within the billing PT's or doctor's discretion.

The Adjuster has a right to expect that the Physical Therapy Claims Reviewer base all observations and judgments directly on the particular documents provided in the case, and that the PT Reviewer be willing to stand by the judgment based on whether or not the claimed treatments were reasonable and necessary parts of a program to restore function. If the review is properly thought through and properly written, the negative findings which led the PT Reviewer to doubt the reasonableness or necessity of care will be understandable and will be readily communicated and readily recalled, if necessary, in a courtroom setting.

The expert who can show that common sense ought to prevail is far more credible than the expert who simply claims to know some specialty better than those untrained in the same specialty. After all, if one PT can claim that, so can another. The PT who filed the bill will have a claim to professional education and to specialized knowledge which could be as strong as that of the PT Reviewer. But if the billing PT failed to use common sense, or failed to document the claim, the court will be justified in ruling to deny that claim.

CHAPTER FIVE ENDNOTES

1. "Soaring Health Care Costs Spur Entrepreneurial Fever--But Surge in Utilization Review Firms May Lead to Shakeout," *Wall Street Journal,* September 6, 1989.
2. Brian Rasmussen, "Claims Review and PTs," *Clinical Management,* January/February, 1990, p. 12.
3. "Medical Tests Go Under the Microscope," *Wall Street Journal,* February 7, 1989.

6 The Role of the Attorney in Cost Containment

Attorney Liaison
Picking a Good Case
Indicators of Success
Start With PIP, First Party or Third Party Cases?
Contributions of the Attorney
Conclusions

THE ROLE OF ATTORNEYS IN COST CONTAINMENT

If an insurance company decides to adopt a serious cost containment or cost management program, it must plan to work closely with qualified and experienced attorneys, who understand both the program and the law. In every jurisdiction, insurance companies work with a group of senior, experienced, and highly competent attorneys who are experts in litigation. However, in choosing a lead attorney with whom to work in cost management in the area of medical and physical therapy claims, the insurance company must be particularly selective. The company will need to attract a dedicated senior attorney who will adopt a long-range commitment to the program. Since many of the cases that arise out of cost containment are small, often in the range of a few hundred dollars, they lack the glamor of the big-issue, high- dollar cases which often attract more senior counsel. Yet, the cases will require significant court experience, as well as a willingness to become intensively familiar with the appropriate law.

The first responsibility of an attorney taking on a leadership role in cost containment is to become familiar with the law and the applicable regulations. Each state and jurisdiction has a different body of pertinent legislation. The attorney should gather copies of the appropriate state laws, any applicable regulations issued by state administrative bodies, and other significant documents. A sensible approach is to copy the law, regulations, rulings of insurance commissioners, pertinent case law, correspondence and copies of letter rulings from professional licensing boards and ethics committees, and to build a file of such materials. In many states, this body of law may fill several binders.

The attorney needs to familiarize himself quite thoroughly with the details of these laws. Just to choose one example, all jurisdictions have specific definitions of the educational requirements for a Registered Physical Therapist, who is qualified to perform certain modalities of treatment. But the degree to which others may practice, and under what types of supervision, varies a great deal: doctors, nurses, licensed practical nurses, physical therapy assistants, physical therapy aides, and other practitioners may or may not be allowed, under individual state laws and regulations, to apply specific modalities.

Each state or jurisdiction will have its own "reasonable and necessary" language in the state insurance codes, which needs to be understood clearly. What constitutes a reasonable charge? What constitutes a necessary treatment? What is the nature of case law and precedent on these questions? Once the attorney is familiar with these specifics, he can begin to fulfill an educational role.

The educational role is fundamental. The attorney needs first to teach himself. Then he must work with the insurance professionals within his client company, teaching the claims supervisors, the claims adjusters and claims investigators, and the higher executives in the firm as well. Once the attorney and the claims personnel have established criteria for identifying problem cases, then the attorney must be willing to work closely to defend the decisions taken by the insurance people if the cases are appropriate.

As discussed in Chapter Three, a number of states provide for some form of first-party coverage, with a Personal Injury Payment (PIP) or an upper limit to a no-fault payment. Whoever is at fault, the injured party will receive payment from his own company to cover the cost of medical treatment and therapy. In those jurisdictions, the insurance company may choose to concentrate on cost containment or cost management on first party cases. Since third party cases often depend upon negotiated settlements in which the crucial factor is not so much the exact or specific amount of the medical or physical therapy billing, but the degree of pain and suffering of the claimant, a close examination of health provider bills does not necessarily result in massive cost containment. In third party cases, much will hinge on how convincing an argument can be made that the injured party endured pain and suffering, quite intangible aspects when compared to the direct bills in the medical special file.

However, in first party claims, the total amount paid out is the total of health provider bills and lost wages. Thus a close examination of the medical specials by the claims review personnel, and the rejection of any inappropriate or inflated amounts there will result in direct savings. Exactly what each state law allows in terms of treatment, modalities, licensing, and what court precedents have been established as to what is reasonable and necessary is thus essential in first party settings.

Insurance policies typically track along with the applicable state law. While everyone may think that they understand exactly what a reasonable charge means, and what necessary care is, the details are often quite complex. One might assume that the treatment must be causally related to the injury. But how is that relationship established and recognized in law? Who is entitled to deliver which particular type of modality of treatment or diagnosis? In most states, it is not "reasonable" for someone to charge for services which they are not trained or licensed to perform. Thus the licensure issue relates to the basic definition of reasonable and necessary care.

What does the law say about physical therapy? In each state there are people called physical therapists, either registered or licensed physical therapists, and the terms are usually used interchangeably. Licensed physical therapists have certain educational requirements. Usually, they are permitted to perform all the various modalities which have been described as typical in this volume. Working with the therapists, are PT assistants. They have to meet certain criteria, and they are permitted to do certain things, which will vary slightly from jurisdiction to jurisdiction. There are physical therapy aides as well. For each of these categories of entitities, there are certain things which each is permitted to do and there are certain things that they are not be permitted to do, either supervised or unsupervised. Clearly, if a class of practitioners is not permitted to perform a certain therapy, they should not be permitted to charge for those services.

Most states have rather specific laws passed by the general assembly or legislative body of the state; in other states some of the details may be covered by administrative rules or regulations, issued by the department of health or another state department. So in addition to the general health code, which applies for all groups of medical practitioners, there may be a body of regulations for each group of practitioners, embodied in the state's code of administrative regulation. Commission rulings and case law may affect exactly how some of the gray area issues are defined. Thus, both types of precedent must be consulted. Furthermore, in many states, active professional associations may enforce their ethical standards with hearings and with letter opinions on specific cases, many of which would prove useful to the thorough attorney. Thus, a knowledge of how the professional groups establish and enforce their own standards, and how state licensing boards review challenged licenses, may also prove essential in building the attorney's files.

Attorney Liaison

Who the attorney works with at the insurance company depends on the size of the office; in the case of a small regional office with a claims officer and one or two adjusters, the attorney would deal with the supervising claims officer. However, for cost containment to be cost-effective, the program should be adopted by the executive level in an insurance company. Thus, the liaison with the attorney will work most effectively if it is established at the executive office of the insurance firm at the state level. The insurance company has to be willing to invest signficiantly more than the individual claim might be worth in order to try it. The company must be willing to try a number of claims in order to set the legal precedents, and to put out the word to the plaintiff's bar and to the providers that limits are to be imposed. To be cost effective, such a program has to be widespread, consistent, legally correct within the jurisdiction, and applied fairly and across the board.

Another reason why the program should be established at the executive office level is because it is there that the relationship between the insurance company and the state insurance commission is maintained. The executive level of the carrier company has to initially agree that cost containment is an important tact to take because in most states, the executive in the carrier's office typically has some relation with the commissioner or whatever regulatory body the state has for dealing with insurance carriers. So somehow, the insurance commissioner has to know what the carrier is doing and why the carrier is doing it. The commissioner must understand that the rejection of claims is part of an appropriate cost-management or cost-containment strategy. This knowledge will reduce potential hostility when the complaints come in. As the program spreads to different parts of the state, the commissioner's staff will become annoyed when it gets lots of complaints from consumers and doctors. The commissioner must understand that the company's approach is to fulfill its obligation to keep the rates down. Of course it is the obligation of the state regulator, the commissioner, to take a look at whether the firm is really keeping the rates down, or whether it is unfairly rejecting claims that it is legally required to pay.

The insurance company considering medical cost management must work with its most experienced and qualified attorneys. A primary potential barrier to success is dealing with the courts. Courts often do not want to be bothered with first party claims, especially in a jurisdiction in which a reasonable cap on the order of a few thousand dollars is maintained on first party claims. Judges who are used to such claims being routinely paid may be quite unsympathetic to the efforts of the insurance company and often sympathize with the plaintiff's side in these lower level proceedings. Furthermore, these small cases take the court's time. The court's predisposition is to require the insurance company to pay the plaintiff-- as that is what insurance companies are in the business for.

> *Commentary*
>
> *Many times, when a judge is unfamiliar with these cases and you start trial, it is like stepping up to the plate, with the count already called at 0 and 2. Sometimes it is even 0 and 3.*
>
> *Leonard Redmond*

Picking a good case

In practice, the medical cost management program will work as follows, with the involvement of a senior attorney. The firm will make a commitment. By selecting from its most experienced attorneys someone willing to take on the legal leadership in the issue. That attorney will study the appropriate and pertinent legislation, regulation, decisions, precedent law, and licensing literature. He or she will educate the claims adjusters, claims supervisiors, and others involved in the firm as to the legal limits and the screening criteria which should be applied. Similarly, a senior person such as a claims superintendent or manager will work closely with the attorney and with the front-line claims people to go through the cases, with a high level of commitment to the program.

Ideally, working with one of the claims offices, the attorney and the senior claims personnel will educate the adjusters and claims people who are familiar with treatment and medical records. The group will meet and decide what specific issues, abuses, and patterns to look at. Furthermore, the insurance company will connect up with physicians and physical therapists, and perhaps with an outside auditing agency or utilization review company to get the medical expertise to support a conclusion of inappropriate billing, either on the basis of poor documentation or on the basis of one of the other criteria described earlier in this text.

Then the carrier will begin to audit the first party files that are identified; have them reviewed by a doctor or by a physical therapist, who would then make recommendations as to whether or not the documentation was adequate, or whether there had been some form of over utilization. When the claims do not meet the criteria, and should be rejected, the carrier goes through the process to notify the attorney for claimant or the provider, that it does not intend to pay the claim.

At that point, the claimants have a chance to argue. The insurance company will have its own criteria as to the point at which it is going to say no. And then, the company should "just say no." Generally, a significant number of those cases in which the insurance company has refused payment will not result in law suits because the plaintiff's lawyer or the physician would not want to be bothered with a lawsuit for several hundred dollars. Naturally, they only want to take on lawsuits that are going to produce a large return. But then the carrier will encounter some lawyers for the plaintiffs, or for the medical providers, who will be willing to be bothered, because they can see what is coming. Suits will be filed.

At that point, the company and its consulting attorney cross another threshold. After the suits are brought, they are sent to the attorney's office for review. The attorney has to make a decision as to whether or not to compromise and settle. Even after the suits are brought, the attorney may decide to compromise and settle a good proportion of them. This is not an area of the law where the attorney should go before the court with 50-50 chance of winning. Rather, the cases that go to court should be those in which the chances of winning appear to be 80 per cent or 90 per cent or better. Good strategy demands that the company go to court only with cases which demonstrate **particularly egregious behavior** on the part of the health care provider.

The reason for that strategy is quite simple. Precisely because there is a range of natural barriers to these cases which make them intrinsicly difficult, the insurance company working with the attorney should only choose to defend the most winnable suits. The "barriers" to winning such cases are several.

For one thing, as already mentioned, many judges do not want to be bothered with small cases. While they may be impressed to discover that the insurance company is bringing its most talented trial lawyers to the cases, and those with the most experience, they may still be reluctant to spend the time involved over a case for a few hundred dollars. A few cases may be lost, or only partially awarded. However, as the details of the cost containment strategy become clear, and as particular patterns of egregious behavior become demonstrated, at some point the judges will begin to become educated.

However, even when the judges have come to understand why and how such cases are being brought, they may still react, as did one judge in a Baltimore District Court, under his breath:

"Oh my God, Not another PIP case!"

When such a judge sees the insurance attorney in the back of court awaiting the turn to take up a PIP case, the judge may take his or her time with the docket in order not to have to hear the case. Inexplicable delays and postponements try the patience of insurance claims personnel, attorneys, as well as the plaintiffs.

The secret of a successful cost containment program is that the lawyer has to take before the court only those cases where there is a substantial chance of winning. Even so, the attorney must expect to loose some of those cases, and the carrier and the adjusters who have invested their time and effort in developing those cases, also must realize that.

Commentary

You walk into court, and you are really wearing a white hat, but you look to everybody else like you are wearing a black hat.

Leonard Redmond

The growth of the "sentinel effect" takes time, and can be set back by loosing cases. However, even when a case is not won in court, the sentinel effect begins to work. Often a win is not for the full amount, but for an adjusted amount such as 75 or 80 cents on the dollar. For a plaintiff's lawyer to spend two to four hours in a district court to win only a few hundred dollars, is not rewarding. Since they have contractual relationships with their health-care provider clients to insure that the bills are being paid, the attoneys are working for no great reward. The plaintiff's attorneys have to spend a great deal of time and money to win 150 or 400 dollars. If the insurance company and its attorney have acted properly, the plaintiff would not be able to claim bad faith. While some jurisdictions might allow award of attorneys' fees, that is a small reward for the work involved in winning such an extensive but small case. Thus, there is a barrier to contesting the cases on the part of the plaintiffs, just as there are barriers to winning them, confronting the defense side.

The insurance carrier must be willing to overcome the severe barriers on its side which include paying for expert witnesses. The expenses for medical personnel and consulting physical therapists in cases which sometimes get postponed, can amount to several thousand dollars for the court supported denial of a claim worth only a few hundred dollars.

In one sense, the insurance company will be able to come out ahead with the working of the sentinel effect from the beginning, because of the funds saved on the uncontested and dropped cases. While few plaintiff's attorneys are eager to take action, once in a while a particular health care provider will decide to sue for payment. Thus, the effort has to be based on a long range strategy, in which the insurance company and its attorney are willing to face a whole series of actions, and be willing to "take a lot of lumps." There may even be actions or hearings brought by the insurance commissioners of the state, or at least meetings in which the policy must be explained and justified. Most junior lawyers would not be prepared to go to district court and deal with the sometimes rough justice that is meted out there, and face, at the same time, the difficult and high-level policy discussions necessary to sustain the cost containment effort with the insurance commission and other state-level investigative bodies.

Both the firm and the attorney have to be committed to the long-range health of the carrier. However, where that has occurred, major carriers have saved substantial amounts, once they have adopted the strategy, and the savings are on-going. Eventually, the savings are reflected in contained rates, a more competitive premium charge, and ultimately, a savings to the general public.

An effective cost containment or cost management program requires a commitment from the top to the bottom of the insurance carrier. The company must not make a half-hearted commitment, because if it does, there are going to be some very rough seas. And similarly, the attorney needs to make a strong commitment. The company may face serious challenge on the commission level in order to make very clear what the program entails: ultimately stopping egregious practices and holding down the cost to the consumer of insurance. Yet such challenges at that level might weaken the knees at the executive level. Similarly, the constant challenge and the setbacks at the level of individual dealing with health care providers and with their attorneys, can weaken the knees of the claims people.

Setbacks are common. It may be discouraging for some of the claims people to settle some of the claims when advised to do so by the attorney. Sometimes the attorney will have to give advice that will not be well received. A case which claims people have carefully considered because it fails to meet the qualifying tests, and because it has a number of flags of abusive over utilization of therapy may have to be paid. The attorney has to make a decision on the kind of evidence and testimony which would be available in a particular case, and decide, from time to time, that if a specific case were lost, it would set back the whole program. Thus, both the attorney and claims people have to be hardened, and be willing to face such decisions. If a medical provider contests a rejected claim, and it is not an egregious case, and the case goes to court and the court awards the payment, then the whole program may be damaged. Credibility with the court and with the commission may be reduced, and the plaintiff's bar may be encouraged to contest further cases. So the decision as to when to litigate and when to negotiate may be a difficult one, but may reflect the recommendation of the attorney which itself is based on a cold look at realistic factors.

Indicators of success in cost containment program

Once a cost containment program is entered into seriously with the necessary long term commitment, eventually the carrier and the attorneys will find evidence of success. The attorney will recognize that he or she is beginning to win cases, to see that the judges are getting educated in the details of medical provider abuses and over-utilization. Another indication of success is that when the number of complaints to the state insurance commissioner begins to increase, and then, the commissioner, in the answers to the complaints, begins to back up the carrier's position. Of course, the insurance company will also have its internal figures, by which it can statistically begin to measure the costs of claims and the costs of engaging in the program.

In several jurisdictions in the early 1990s, several of the more progressive insurance companies have adopted such programs, and are well aware that they are beginning to work. Particularly those companies which have focussed in cost management in first-party, PIP or MEDPAY claims growing out of auto liability policies, in which there is high-volume litigation, can identify marked success in reducing claims.

Why start with PIP or first party, rather than third party cases?

It may seem counter-intuitive for insurance companies to begin their cost containment efforts in the auto liability area in the first party, PIP or MED PAY area. If the settlements in third party cases, by a rough rule of thumb are worth two and a half to five times the cost of medicals and lost wages, why not focus first on such more expensive cases? The reasons for a focus on payments under PIP or MED PAY, are several.

The system often works thus. An individual in a PIP or MED PAY state who has an accident resulting in only soft-tissue injury will go to an attorney. The attorney will refer the patient for a round of medical and physical therapy treatments, to a group of specialists with whom the attorney is familiar. These practitioners know that they will be paid by the injured party's own insurance company, under and up to the no-fault limit of an amount like $3000 or $5000, depending on the local jurisdiction. The physicians and therapists will provide services at or slightly above that limit, accepting for payment the individual's assignment of the bill to his own carrier for the PIP or MED PAY payment.

The principle of such coverage is well-intended. Injured parties receive immediate treatment; the doctors and therapists receive prompt payment of all or most of their bills, and the question of liability is left for the more drawn out, and often negotiated third-party claim in which the first party's insurance claim is resolved by a decision as to was the wrong-doer. Under the circumstances of a PIP payment, the carrier's only payment is the direct cost of the medical claim. If the insurance company scrutinizes such claims in soft-tissue injuries, and carefully identifies those cases which clearly indicate over-utilization, inappropriate treatment, or inadequate documentation, and rejects those claims, it will send a message out to the health care provider community that only legitimate care will be reimbursed. That will create an immediate sentinel effect.

Then, as some of those cases are brought forth for litigation, a further message is sent. A certain proportion of these hard-fought cases will be won, a certain proportion lost. If the attorney and the carrier are careful to only go to litigation on the most egregious cases, the plaintiff's bar and the health care providers will take notice. In some jurisdictions, some of the notoriously over-charging clinics have been driven from business; others begin to curtail their abuses. Practices such as using unlicensed individuals to deliver inappropriate modalities; the importation of a physician or therapist from another jurisdiction to sign off on work done by a nurse or an aid; or the stacking and overcharging for modalities sharply decline; spurious and scientifically undemonstrated modalities have been eliminated from coverage.

As reviewed in Chapter Three, in some states, denial of first party claims represents a much greater risk for the carrier than in others. In some states, if the court decides that a claim was legitimate, the carrier may face the risk of paying punitive damages, based upon an additional claim that the carrier acted in bad faith in its contractual relationship with its client, the insured party. In order to file for punitive damages in some states, the claimant must prove actual malice, not simple negligence. In such states, the carrier is protected from a punitive damage claim, as long as it can demonstrate that it made an honest appraisal of the claim, and that it equitably and fairly applied standard criteria to the claim before rejecting it. However, not all states make such a distinction, and the contract law as applied to insurance companies varies considerably from state to state.

Such variation in state laws makes it crucial and essential that a carrier consult with its most highly qualified attorneys before deciding what approach to take in cost containment. The highest policy decision must be made: in some jurisdictions it is quite appropriate and effective to challenge first party PIP or MED PAY claims when they reflect an inappropriate medical provider billing; in other jurisdictions, cost containment may be more safely and reasonably applied only in a third-party setting.

In a sense, cost containment spreads as matter of education. The insurance company claims adjuster, when educated, begins to contain the costs. He begins to pay only for proper diagnosis and proper treatment; as we have seen, he may begin with a process that contains the first party costs. Thus, the adjuster will also be trained as a solid negotiator for third party cases. Judges will begin to throw out claims when they too have been educated, as they begin to understand the issues of certification, documentation, types of modality, and the various unethical forms of overbilling through excessive treatment and duplicative billing. The process begins to spread from the lead attorney, through the claims adjusters, to the other attorneys, and more widely through the insurance practice in the state.

Contributions of the Attorney to Cost Containment

Beyond his role as educator, litigator, negotiator, and consultant, the experienced attorney in the cost containment program can provide practical individualized knowledge upon which tactical decisions can be made. For example, through his knowledge of the medical and physical therapy practitioners in a region, the attorney can help identify those physicians and physical therapists who are "entrepreneurial" in their orientation, for whom a high-dollar volume is more crucial than accurate diagnosis or appropriate treatment. When the attorney receives a group of claims which have been identified by the adjusters or by utilization review to indicate problems, he can apply his practical first hand knowledge of various clinics, physicians, and physical therapists in the region. Knowing their reputation in the community, and knowing in detail the way in which they practice, the attorney can help identify the weak spots in their documentation.

Furthermore, the attorney must have a subtle and experienced background in litigation, for the issues are sensitive, and can readily backfire. Often court battles can become quite unpleasant, and the attorney must not only have the skills of a diplomat, but must also have a thick skin. In some cases, especially those involving a jury, it may seem as if the carrier's attorney is unfairly picking on the doctor. After all, the injured individual sought medical treatment; the doctor or the physical therapist did provide service; now, it appears, the insurance company is balking at paying a charge for which it is obligated. The attorney must be able to demonstrate that the charge was not reasonable or necessary, and it must be shown that the attorney is not unfairly picking on the doctor. Often, the exchanges require a subtle touch; for if it appears that the physical therapist's own professional judgement is being challenged unfairly, the attorney could easily annoy the jury or the judge. In effect, the carrier's attorney has to accuse the doctor or the physical therapist of running up the bill in an inappropriate fashion; to make such an accusation without excellent and clear documentation in a convincing manner can seem callous and disrespectful to another professional.

Dealing with expert witnesses calls upon special skills. The attorney must advise the insurance carrier to carefully select their expert witnesses. Often the Independent Medical Examiners and other experts brought by the carrier will have a reputation or appear to be "hired guns," that is, simply paid to say whatever it is that the carrier would like them to say. Thus, the selection of experts during a serious cost-containment program should engage the advice and experience of the attorney. To an extent it is a classic problem: how does one match the qualifications of one expert against those of another? Ideally, the expert witness is highly qualified in his own field, with an established reputation and a continuing practice, outside of simply appearing to testify. The motivation for the expert's testifying should go beyond his or her fee; the expert should have and be able to demonstrate a repute for demanding professional standards within the appropriate practitioner groups. That training, background, experience, and qualification should be made clear in the *voir dire* section of the testimony.

Furthermore, the expert should not be simply there to present a report. Rather, he or she should understand that the appropriate role, like that of the attorney, is to educate. The expert needs to show exactly what each modality is for, how it is used properly, what the professional standards say as to who is to use it and how it is to be used, and how its use should be documented. Working from the documentation available, the expert should be able to make it clear what contradictions or gaps in the record provided by the plaintiff's side led to the conclusion that the modality was inappropriate, unreasonable, or unnecessary. If done well, the expert's testimony will make clear to the judge and or jury exactly why, from a professional viewpoint, it would not be correct to pay for treatment after a certain point, or for a certain set of treatments. The logic spelled out in Chapter Five, describing the claims review process, should become obvious and clear to judge and jury. The attorney, in preparing the expert for testimony needs to make it clear to the expert that an educational role is expected, and that both judges and juries are hungry for rich and detailed information. A degree of technical information must be imparted for a person with a general background; it must be sophisticated enough to allow the layman to understand exactly what is at stake. Thus the carrier must be willing to spend the money that it takes to have the attorney consult with the expert witness and to develop and train that witness so that he or she can make the most convincing and worthwhile presentation.

The attorney must demonstrate to the fact finder that the carrier's expert is educated, and motivated by a concern for a maintaining good standards in the profession. To an extent, the "battle of credentials" is won or lost, not simply on comparing schools, experience, age, and practice, but on how the carrier's expert testimony sounds as compared to the plaintiff's expert. In effect, it is a test of how well the expert teaches.

Even in an ideal situation, the plaintiff has a built-in advantage, since the billing practitioner can say: I saw the patient, and in my professional judgement, such and such a treatment was called for. "I saw, I touched, I decided, I treated." The critic has to point to the record and respond: From the record provided at the time of the examination and treatment, these are the problems. And that must be followed by a thorough, convincing, and accurate analysis of why there was a problem.

Ultimately the bottom line in litigating these cases is that the insurance carrier must only go to trial with those cases that reflect the most egregious practices. And even with that pre-selection, the insurance carrier must be willing to settle some of the cases. Such an approach requires that the carrier have intestinal fortitude. Both the carrier and the attorney have to be willing to see this as a long range, long term problem; neither can expect that it will be easy in the short run.

An undesired consequence of all of the education and all of the sentinel effect is that the carrier may be educating the other side; unscrupulous providers simply learn how to cheat better and to present more convincing documentation. In fact, groups of medical practitioners frequently request meetings with insurance companies engaged in cost management asking, "Tell us how you want us to do it." The response from the carriers has to be: simply provide professional treatment to reasonable and necessary extents, and you will be properly reimbursed.

Both the attorneys and the carriers must work closely with auditing firms, and that relationship must not be too incestuous. Attorneys must assist in making it clear to utilization review firms that they have a separate identity and a fee structure that does not simply pay them more for the more problems they discover. The carriers and the utilization review firms must avoid collusion, and even the appearance of collusion.

Like expert witnesses, they too must be independent. Preferably, the utilization review firm should be able to demonstrate that it has sometimes recommended full payment of claims. However, as carriers develop their own "screens" and "screening criteria lists" to identify problem claims, and if the carriers refer only such problem cases to utilization review firms for examination, it becomes more and more reasonable that a very high proportion of the cases reviewed are recommended for denial of claim. Nevertheless, the attorney should be in a position to insist that no collusive relationship between the "UR" firm and the carrier exists.

In some jurisdictions, for a utilization review firm to reject 100 per cent of the claims referred for review might serve as evidence of "reckless disregard," and represent a form of legal malice which would open the carrier to a claim for punitive damages. Thus, in its use of UR firms as well as expert witnesses, the carrier should seek the advice of counsel to avoid opening itself inadvertently to unexpected suits.

Conclusions

In order for the long-range sentinel effect to work, the carrier must establish that it is not a pushover. The insurance company, working with its consulting attorney, has to recognize that the majority of the claims that are rejected never go to court: some are dropped by the provider; in others the provider's lawyer is too lazy and suit is never filed; or the provider accepts the cut. Other cases go to negotiation for settlement. A small proportion of the cases that are rejected result in suits; a small proportion of those suits must however be fought all the way, and ideally that small proportion should demonstrate the most egregious practices on the part of the health care providers. And in that small number of cases, the presence of a high quality, well-informed, good trial lawyer is essential. The overall success of the program will result from the fact that the sheer rejection of inappropriate claims will immediately result in savings.

In those jurisdictions in which the cases can be structured so that the claimant is the physical therapist or other health care provider, rather than the insured individual, the carrier can reduce the built-in odds against success. Juries and judges to an extent believe that insurance companies have deep pockets. Both judges and juries are for that reason disposed to award funds to the "little guy," when he is up against a large corporation. But that predeliction is reduced when the claimant is a clinic or other health care provider. And if it can be demonstrated that the clinic operates in a gray area of ethics, the disposition to settle for the plaintiff can evaporate.

A few cases, in which the carrier can come to the defense of the injured party and defend the accident victim from suit by the health care provider, have been ideal cases in which to exercise cost containment. However, such cases are rare, and have become even more rare, as the health care providers come to understand how difficult it is to win against a cost-containing firm who happens to appear in court on the side of the ultimate little guy, the accident victim.

Attorneys will advise the carriers to take only the cases that they are likely to win, and even then, to face the fact that they are going to loose some. Such an approach lets the provider community know that the carrier is serious; secondly, it tends to educate the judges and the plaintiff's bar; eventually, the approach will be appreciated by the general public. However, providers begin to lobby and work through the state legislatures. It will become the responsiblity of attorneys, claims personnel, and others engaged in cost containment, to translate the motives and goals of their policy not only for the state insurance commissions, but for the media, the public, and for the state legislatures, so that cost containment can be seen as in the general interest. Those in cost containment have to overcome the burden that the insurance carrier is regarded as obligated to pay. First, one must educate the adjusters, then educate the bench, then educate the plaintiffs, and finally, move to educating the ultimate victim of over-utilization, the general public and the insurance rate payer.

The attorney selected by the insurance carrier needs to familiarize himself with the law and with the modalities; he or she must be prepared to walk into a hostile environment; expect it and anticipate it. Furthermore, the attorney has to have the seniority, experience, and conviction to be able to successfully convince the client not to proceed in certain cases. Sometimes, once cost containment gets underway and the duplicity involved in over utilization becomes more widely understood, some personnel in the insurance carrier may become be blinded by anger. They may loose sight of the big picture, because they feel a commitment to deny a particular case. One over-billing which they regard as egregious may in fact be difficult to demonstrate or prove; the evidence or the particular jurisdiction or judge may not be tacticly adviseable. In those cases, the attorney needs to be prepared to make a firm stand; the carrier needs to be able to take such difficult advice and stand down from the particular battle in order to win the longer range goal. Both sides need to be realistic.

If a carrier is using a credible cost containment process, the attorneys have to understand that it is winnable and defensible. Carriers have to go to defense attorneys and select the best and most effective advocates. It may fall on the attorneys to lead the charge.

Commentary
Snake oil by any other name is still snake oil.
Leonard Redmond

The battle for cost containment is one that runs into the pitfalls of human nature at every turn. Accident victims naturally make up for their sense of misfortune by seeing in the accident an opportunity to make money, to partially redress their sense of frustration that fate acted against them. They seek the advice of attorneys, physicians, and physical therapists. In cases of the marginal soft tissue injury, it is not at all hard to start to believe that the treatment and therapy was necessary and helpful. Palliative treatment does indeed make one feel better, if only temporarily. Role playing as patient can be a small compensation for the pain. Entrepreneurial physicians and entrepreneurial physical therapists are perfectly adept at taking advantage of these all-too-human needs. Some simply stretch the definition of necessary and reasonable treatment to whatever they think the limits of coverage will provide. Others verge over the line into unethical or even fraudulent treatment, and definitely should not be able to get away with the practices.

Individuals pay premiums to insurance companies, and most individuals either feel that they personally, or someone they know, have been the victims of large enterprises in the society, of which insurance companies are typical. Multi-million dollar corporations denying an individual some small compensation for medical treatment incurred through an accident seem particularly villainous at first glance. Judges, juries, and outside observers find it easy to cast the large enterprise in the role of villain, the injured party or plaintiff in the role of victim. Unfortunately, human affairs are never as simple as the good and evil of melodrama.

In reality, the mix of motivations makes such transactions and treatments far more complex in each individual case. In the aggregate the thousands of cases of injury and compensation which flow through the claims departments of insurance carriers represent a great range of ethical, legal, medical, psychological, and financial factors.

Within a legal framework, the insurance carriers have differing responsibilities which, to an extent, act at cross purposes. They must compensate for reasonable and necessary medical coverage in cases of injury. At the same time, they are obliged to restrain the rising cost of insurance premiums by identifying inappropriate, unreasonable and unnecessary practice where they can. To the extent that such costs can be controlled, the carriers also act in the public interest.

To do that effectively must engage the efforts of all involved. They must be willing to practically assist in identifying the cases, establishing the precedents and the case law, and in taking the heat as the battles are fought out in the courts.

Appendices

1. Physical Therapy Guidelines 109
2. Abbreviations in common use 115
3. CPT Codes 119
4. Normal Range of Motion, in Degrees 125
5. Physical Therapy Modalities 126

APPENDIX 1
PHYSICAL THERAPY GUIDELINES

The following guidelines are based on medicare guidelines for screening outpatient Physical Therapy, on surveys and interviews with specialists in the field, and on our own experience reviewing thousands of claims.

I. GUIDELINE: APPROVAL OF CARE

Care should be approved:
- if physical therapy is indicated by diagnosis or loss of function
- documentation showed significant progress within a reasonable period of time (see Table, below)
- duration and frequency of treatment was reasonable (see Table, below)
- skilled services of a physical therapist were needed and provided

II. GUIDELINE: DENIAL OF CARE

Additional care should be denied if
- no significant progress within a reasonable period of time
- frequency and duration unreasonable for the injury or condition
- skilled physical therapy not required because the delivered modality did not require skill; or not required because of palliative or maintenance care
- patient progress has plateaued; exercises repetitive with no objective improvement; patient shows no rehabilitation potential; no further significant functional improvement can be reasonably expected. If objective findings of strength remain the same for 2 to 3 weeks, then Physical Therapy was not effective.
- On-going care on an as-needed basis is not acceptable.

III. GUIDELINE: SKILLED CARE

Extended non-skilled care should not be covered. Skilled physical therapy service can be performed only by Registered or Licensed Physical Therapist or under direct supervision of Physical Therapist. (Or in those states in which physicians are licensed to perform PT, by or under the supervision of a physician.) Indications of non- skilled care are:
- exercise program taught to patient is repetitive and/or exercise have become maintenance
- patient has plateaued or does not show improvement in objective findings
- when exercise is given by non-skilled personnel; when the modality is appropriately self-applied.
- when exercises can be done as part of a home program

Physical therapy modalities are skilled when given as integral part of skilled treatment and followed by therapeutic exercises or other activities to increase range of motion, strength or function resulting from disease or injury.

IV. GUIDELINE: TREATMENT FOR PAIN

With soft tissue injuries, the goal is to relieve pain so as to increase range of motion, strength or function. The mere presence of subjective complaints of pain does not necessarily indicate a need for skilled physical therapy services, particularly if the pain resulting from injury does not directly result in functional impairment or limitation of posture, strength, or mobility. Records justifying treatment for pain should describe presence or absence of pain and its effect on the patient's functions and abilities.

V. GUIDELINE: DEFINITIONS OF REASONABLE NUMBER, FREQUENCY, DURATION OF TREATMENTS

It should be noted that in order to apply these guidelines, working definitions of reasonable numbers of visits, reasonable frequency of visits, and reasonable duration of treatment for a particular injury are appropriate. In the table below we provide general guidelines on number, frequency and duration; particular traumas, with the specific appropriate Frequency, Number of Visits, and Duration in weeks. In most cases treatment of soft tissue injury beyond four to six weeks should be supported by documentation of functional impairment in objective, measurable terms.

The guidelines as to duration and frequency are based on a variety of published standards and upon observation of common and typical practices. The insurance professional should be sure to understand that these guidelines are not intended as set limits, but rather, the figures should serve as a guide to the approximate typical length and frequency of treatments for various injuries and conditions. By themselves these figures should not be interpreted as setting any upper or lower limits; only a professional judgement based upon particular circumstances can determine a proper course of treatment.

The reader will note that the range of total treatments provided in the table below sometimes includes a minimum figure which is higher than the multiple of the lowest per week frequency and the minimum indicated total weeks of treatment. Similarly, the maximum of the total indicated may be lower than the multiple of highest per week frequency and longest duration. The reason for these apparent discrepancies is that treatment is conventionally more frequent in the earlier weeks, tapering off in later weeks. Thus, for example, a treatment indicated at the rates of two or three times a week for ten to twelve weeks, may typically average 24 to 30 total visits, rather than the lower and higher seemingly possible multiples of 20 to 36. The patient may begin at the rate of three times a week, running for four weeks (12 total visits) and then taper off to 2 visits a week for another six weeks. In such a case of good progress, the total would be 24 visits, an approximate minimum for the particular treatment. A rate of three times a week for six weeks (18 visits) coupled another six weeks of two visits each would bring the total to 30 visits, the approximate typical maximum for this treatment.

In any case, however, the totals indicated here are to be considered only general

APPENDIX 1 PHYSICAL THERAPY GUIDELINES 111

guidelines; many circumstances legitimately call for more extensive or frequent treatment. The insurance claims reviewer should seek documentation to explain the non-typical cases which exceed these generally common patterns.

TABLE OF FREQUENCY, NUMBER, AND DURATION OF TREATMENTS

These are the most common soft tissue and trauma related injuries. The list is not inclusive of all aspects of physical therapy care, but is meant to encompass the majority of patients treated with trauma-related, soft tissue injuries on an out-patient basis. There are many other conditions and diagnoses that legitimately require physical therapy. These are the injuries most likely to involve over-utilization of physical therapy services.

If claim exceeds the limits shown: obtain and review progress reports and Physical Therapy notes. Approve more care if:

1] objective findings present
2] findings show significant improvement in a reasonable period of time

When additional care is approved, it should be limited to 2 to 3 times per week for 2 to 4 weeks, only if skilled Physical Therapy still required, not just palliative treatments (such as hot packs or electrical stimulation).

INJURY/SEVERITY FACET	FREQUENCY PER WEEK	TOTAL NUMBER OF VISITS	DURATIONS OF SYNDROME (TOTAL IN WEEKS)
NECK			
Cervical strain/sprain mild/moderate	2-3	12-18	4-6
Trauma whiplash (Severe Cervical strain with radiating pain; radiculpathy; radiculitis)	2-3	16-24	6-8
HNP, Bulging disc symptomatic & diagnostic testing	2-3	24-30	10-12
degenerative disc	2-3	12-18	4-6
Catchall terms:	2-3	12-18	4-6

INJURY/SEVERITY FACET	FREQUENCY PER WEEK	TOTAL NUMBER OF VISITS	DURATION OF SYNDROME (TOTAL IN WEEKS)
myofascitis, myositis, fibromyositis			
LOW BACK			
Lumbar back strain/sprain T-L, L-S, S-1	2-3	12-18	4-6
mild-moderate	2-3	12-18	4-6
severe	2-3	16-24	6-8
sciatic	2-3	18-28	8-10
Intervertebral disc disorders HNP disc herniation	2-3	24-30	10-12
Degenerative disc--severe (note: operative procedures)	2-3	12-18	4-6

FRACTURES
Require more rehabilitation, must be supported by objective findings of limited range of motion and strength.

CARPAL TUNNEL post surgical	3	12-18	4-6
SHOULDER			
sprain/strain	3	12-18	4-6
ac separation/dislocation	3	12-18	4-6
rotator cuff	3	16-24	6-8
adhesive capsulitis	3	24-30	8-10
ELBOW			
sprain/strain rupture/tear	3	12-18	4-6
dislocation	3	16-24	6-8
WRIST			
sprain/strain	3	8-12	2-4

APPENDIX 1 PHYSICAL THERAPY GUIDELINES

INJURY/SEVERITY FACET	FREQUENCY PER WEEK	TOTAL NUMBER OF VISITS	DURATION OF SYNDROME (TOTAL IN WEEKS)
CONTUSIONS			
elbow-arm	3	8-12	2-4
leg-hip-knee-ankle	2-3	8-12	2-4
ARTHRALGIA OR JOINT PAIN	2-3	8-12	2-4
MUSCULAR STRAIN			
Quad, Hamstring, gastroc	2-3	8-12	2-4
HIP			
strain/sprain	2-3	12-18	4-6
dislocation	2-3	20-36?	10-12
KNEE			
strain/sprain (no ligamentous tears)	2-3	12-18	4-6
knee-internal derangement meniscus and ligament-non-surgical	2-3	12-24	6-8
post-operative artroscopy-meniscectomy	2-3	8-12	2-4
ligamentous/medial collateral	2-3	24-30	8-10
ACL-strain and repair	2-3	30-36	12-16

Post operative rehab often reqiures longer treatment but is easily documented by objective findings.

ANKLE			
sprain-grade 1 & 2 mild to moderate	2-3	8-12	2-4
severe-grade 3	2-3	12-18	4-6
Fx closed-post-casting	2-3	8-12	2-4

INJURY/SEVERITY FACET	FREQUENCY PER WEEK	TOTAL NUMBER OF VISITS	DURATION OF SYNDROME (TOTAL IN WEEKS)
Fx bimalleolar	2-3	12-18	4-6
FOOT			
Sprain and contusion	2-3	8-12	2-4

Appendix 2
Abbreviations in Common Use

a	before
A	assessment
AA	automobile accident
AAROM	active assistive range of motion
AC	acromioclavicular joints
ad libat	discretion
ADL	activities of daily living
adm	admission
AE	above elbow
AFO	ankle foot orthosis
AIIS	anterior inferior iliac spine
AJ	ankle jerk
Ak	above knee
alt	alternate
alt die	alternate days
am	morning
AP	anterior-posterior
AROM	active range of motion
ASA	aspirin
ASAP	as soon as possible
ASIS	anterior superior iliac spine
assist.	assistant assistance
B/S	bedside
BE	below elbow
bid	twice a day
bin	twice a night
bis	twice
BK	below knee
BP	blood pressure
bpm	beats per minute
BR	bedrest
BRP	bathroom privileges
c/o	complains of
CA	carcinoma, cancer
CAD	coronary artery disease
cal	calories
CBC	complete blood count
CC, C/C	chief complaint
CCW	counterclockwise
CHF	congestive heart failure
cm	centimeter
CNS	central nervous system
COLD	chronic obstructive lung disease
CONT.	continue
COPD	chronic obstructive pulmonary disease
COTA	certified occupational therapy assistant
CP	cerebral palsy
CPR	cardiopulmonary resuscitation
CV	cardiovascular
CVA	cerebrovascular accident
CW	clockwise
CWI	crutch walking instructions
D/C	discontinue, discontinued or discharged
D.C.	doctor of chiropractic
decr	decrease
dept.	department
DF	dorsiflexion
DIP	distal interphalangeal joint
DISC	discontinue
disch	discharge
DM	diabetes mellitis
DO	doctor of osteopathy
DTR	deep tendon reflex
Dx	diagnosis
E.R.	emergency room
ECF	extended care facility
ECG, EKG	electrocardiogram
EEG	electroencephalogram
EMG	electromyogram
ER	external rotation
ES	external stimulation
eval	evaluation
EX, Ex	exercise

EXT, Ext	extension	IV	intravenous
F	fair (muscle strength, balance)	jt, jnt	joint
FCE	functional capacity evaluation		
fes	functional electircal stimulation	kcal	kilocalories
		kg	kilogram
FH	family history	KJ	knee jerk
FLEX	flexion		
freq	frequent	l	[circled]left
ft.	foot, feet (the measurement, not the body part)	L.,	l.liter or left
		lb.	pound
FWB	full weight bearing	LBP	low back pain
Fx	fracture	LE	lower extremity
		LOC	loss of consciousness
G	good (muscle strength, balance)	LP	lumbar puncture
GI	gastrointestinal		
gm	gram	m	meter
GRAD	gradually, by degrees	M&R	measure and record
		MD	medical doctor; doctor c medicine
h, hr.	hour		
H & P	history and physical	Meds.	medications
HA, H/A	headache	MFT	muscle function test
HBP	high blood pressure	mg	milligram
HEENT	head, ear, eyes, nose, throat	MH	moist heat
EP	home exercise program	MI	myocardial infarction
HNP	herniated nucleus pulposus	min.	minutes
HO	history of	mm	millimeter
HP	hot pack	MMT	manual muscle testing
HR	heart rate	mo.	month
hr.	hour	MOB	mobilization
ht.	height	MP, MCP	metacarpalphalangeal
Htn	hypertension	MS	multiple sclerosis
Hx,	hxhistory	MVA	motor vehicle accident
ICTx	intermittent cervical traction	N	normal (muscle strengtl
ICU	intensive care unit	N.H.	nursing home
id	the same	NDT	neurodevelopmental treatment
IM	intramuscular		
imp.	impression	neg.	negative
in d	daily	noc	night, at night
in.	inches	noct	at night
Incr	increase	NPO	nothing by mouth
IPTx	intermittent pelvic traction	NWB	non weight bearing
IR	internal rotation	O.P.	outpatient

APPENDIX 2 ABBREVIATIONS IN COMMON USE

O.R.	operating room	q	every
O:	objective	q2h	every two hours
Occ	occasional	q3h	every three hours
om	every morning	q4h	every four hours
OOB	out of bed	qd	every day
ORIF	open reduction, internal fixation	qh	every hour
		qhs	every bedtime
OT	occupational therapist, occupational therapy	qid	four times a day
		ql	as much as desired
oz.	ounce	qm	every morning
		qn	every night
P	poor, after, or position	qod	every other day
P.A.	physician's assistant	qqhor	every hour
P.H.	past history	qv	as much as you like
P:	plan (treatment plan)		
PA	posterior/anerior	(r)	right
para	paraplegia	R	right
pc	after meals	RA	rheumatoid arthritis
per	by/through	re:	regarding
PF	plantar flexion	REF	refer
PMHX	past medical history	reps	repetitions
PNF	proprioceptive neuromescular facilitation	resp	respiratory, respiration
		R.O.	rule out (In order to make a good diagnosis, the physician will try to rule the named disease/condition out; if he or she cannot, this will become the diagnosis.)
PNI	peripheral nerve injury		
PO	postoperative		
POMR	problem-oriented medical record		
pos.	positive		
poss	possible		
post-op	after surgery (operation)	ROM	range of motion
PRE	progressive resistive exercise	ROS	review of systems
pre-op	before surgery (operation)	Rot	rotate
prn	whenever necessary	RROM	resistive range of motion
PROM	passive range of motion	RT	right
PSIS	posterior superior iliac spine	RX, Rx	treatment, prescription, therapy
PT	physical therapy, physical therapist		
Pt., pt.	patient	s̄	without
pta	prior to admission	S	label, left, sign, without
PTA	physical therapy assistant	S.P., S/P	status post (recent past)
PTB	patellar tendon bearing	SACH	solid ankle cushion heel
PVD	peripheral vascular disease	SC	jointsternoclavicular joint
PWB	partial weight bearing	sec.	seconds
		SI(J)	sacroiliac (joint)

sig	directions for use, give as follows, let it be labeled	wk.	week
SLR	straight leg raise	WNL	within normal limits
SNF	skilled nursing facility	wt.	weight
SOAP	subjective, objective, assessment, plan	x	number of times performed (X2 = twice, X3 = three)
SOB	shortness of breath		
spec	specimen	y/o	years old
stat	immediately, at once	yd.	yard
STM	soft tissue mobilization	yr.	year
Sx	symptoms		
		+1, +2	assistance (assistance of 1 or 2 persons given; also written "assistance of 1")
T	trace (muscle strength)		
t.o.	telephone order tbsp. tablespoon	♀	male
		♂	female
TENS, TNS	transcutaneous electrical nerve stimulator	↓	down, downward, decrease
		↑	up, upward, increase
THR	total hip replacement	//	parallel or parallel bars (also written //bars)
tid	three times daily		
TKR	total knee replacement		
TLC	tender loving care	@	with
TM(J),TMJ	temporomandibular (joint)	w/o	without
TNR	tonic neck reflex (also ATNR, STNR)	>	greater than
		<	less than
TO	telephone order	=	equals
TPR	temperature, pulse, & respiration	+	plus, positive (circled)
		-	minus, negative (circled)
tsp.	teaspoon	#	number; pounds
		/	per
UE	upper extremity	%	percent
UNK	unknown	+,&,et	and
URI	upper respiratory infection		
US	ultrasound		
UV	ultraviolet		
v.o., V/O	verbal orders		
v.s.	vital signs		
VMO	vastus medialis oblique		
w/c	wheelchair		
W/cm²	watts per square centimeter		
WBAT	weight bearing as tolerated		
WBC	white blood cell count		
WFL	within functional limits		
WH	work hardening		

Appendix 3

Current Procedures Terminology [CPT] Codes
For Selected Physical Therapy Services

Modalities	CPT	Procedures	CPT
Hot or Cold packs	97010	One area, initial 30 mins.	
Traction, mechanical	97012	Therapeutic exercise	97110
Electrical stim. (unattn'd)	97014	Neuromuscular re-education	97112
Vasopneumatic devices	97016	Functional Activities	97114
Paraffin bath	97018	Gait training	97116
Microwave	97020	Electrical stimulation	97118
Whirlpool	97022	Iontophoresis	97120
Diathermy	97024	Traction, manual	97122
Infrared	97026	Massage	97124
Ultraviolet	97028	Contrast baths	97126
Unlisted modality, specify	97039	Ultrasound	97128
Office visit, 2 modalities	M0005[1]	Unlisted procedure, specify	97139
additional 15 mins.	M0006[1]	Treatment, one area	
Office visit, comb. mod.	M0007[1]	Each Additional 15 mins.	97145
additional 15 mins.	M0008[1]		
Therapy Services		Tests and Measures	
Hubbard tank, initial 30 mins.	97220	Office visit for orthotic,	
additional 15 mins.	97221	prosthetic, and daily living	
w/exercise, initial 30 mins.	97240	check-out, initial 30 mins.	97700
additional 15 mins.	97241	additional 15 mins.	97701
Orthotics training,		Extremity (one)	97720
initial 30 mins.	97500	additional 15 mins.	97721
additional 15 mins.	97501	Muscle testing	97752
Prosthetic training,		Unlisted, service or	
initial 30 mins.	97520	procedure	97799
additional 15 mins.	97521	Training in Activities	
Kinetic activity,		of Daily Living	97540
initial 30 mins.	97530	additional 15 mins.	97541
additional 15 mins.	97531		

Source: 1993 *Physician's Current Procedural Terminology*, AMA Fourth Ed., AMA, 1993.

Neurology and Neuromuscular Procedures

Modalities	CPT	Procedures	CPT
Electromography, one Muscle testing, manual; extremity or trunk			
with report	95831		
hand	95833		
Total evaluation of body, excluding hands	95833		
Total evaluation of body, including hands	95834		
Muscle testing, electrica	95842		
Range of motion measurements and report; each		Electromyography, limited study of specific	
extremity, excluding hand	95851	muscles	95869
hand	95852		
extremity and related paraspinal areas	95860		
two extremities	95861		
three extremities	95863		
four extremities	95864		

Source: 1993 Physician's Current Procedural Terminology, AMA Fourth Ed., AMA, 1993.

CPT CODES FOR OTHER SERVICES

Physical Medicine 96900-97020

In addition, services and skills outlined under Evaluation and Management levels of service appropriate to dermatologic illinesses should be coded similarly. (For intralesional injections, see 11900, 11901)
(For Tzanck smear, use 87207)

- 96900 Actinotherapy (ultraviolet light)
- 96910 Photochemotherapy; tar and ultraviolet B (Goeckerman treatment) or petrolatum and ultraviolet B
- 96912 psolarlens and ultraviolet A (PUVA)
- 96913 Photochemotherapy (Goerckerman and/or PUVA) for severe photoresponsive dermatoses requiring at least four to eight hours of care under direct supervision of the physician (includes application of medication and dressings)
- 96999 Unlisted special dermatological service or procedure

PHYSICAL MEDICINE

(Performed or supervised by physician)
(For muscle testing, range of joint motion, electromyography, see 95831 et seq)
(For biofeedback training by EMG, see 90900)
(For trancutaneous nerve stimulation (TNS), see 64550)

MODALITIES

(Physician or therapist is required to be in constant attendance)
(97000 has been deleted. To report, use 97010-97039)

- 97010 Physical medicine treatment to one area; hot or cold packs
- 97012 traction, mechanical
- 97014 electrical stimulation (unattended)
- 97016 vasopneumatic devices
- 97018 parrafin bath
- 97020 microwave
- 97022 whirlpool
- 97024 diathermy
- 97026 infrared
- 97028 ultraviolet
- 97039 unlisted modality (specify)

PROCEDURES

(Physician or therapist is required to be in constant attendance)

(97100 has been deleted. To report, use 97110-97139)

(97101 has been deleted. To report, use 97145)

97110	Physical medicine treatment to one area, initial 30 minutes, each visit; therapeutic exercises
97112	neuromuscular reeducation
97114	functional activities
97116	gait training
97118	electrical stimulation (manual)
97120	iontopheresis
97122	traction, manual
97124	massage
97126	contrast baths
97128	ultrasound
97139	unlisted procedure (specify)
97145	Physical medicine treatment to one area, each additional 15 minutes

(97200, 97201 have been deleted. To report, see 97010-97039, 97110-97145)

97220	Hubbard tank; initial 30 minutes, each visit
97221	each additional 15 minutes, up to one hour
97240	Pool therapy or Hubbard tank with therapeutic exercises; initial 30 minutes, each visit
97241	each additional 15 minutes, up to one hour
97260	Manipulation (cervical, thoracic, lumboscaral, sacroiliac, hand, wrist) (separate procedure), performed by physician; one area
97261	each additional area

(for manipulation under general anesthesia, see appropriate anatomic section in Musuloskeletal System)

97500	Orthotics training (dynamic bracing, splinting), upper and/or lower extremities; initial 30 minutes, each visit
97501	each additional 15 minutes

(codes 97500, 97501 should not be reported with 97116)

97520	Prosthetic training; initial 30 minutes, each visit
97521	each additional 15 minutes

APPENDIX 3 CPT CODES   123

97530	Kinetic activities to increase coordination, strenth and/or range of motion, one area (any two extremities or trunk); initial 30 minutes, each visit
97531	each additional 15 minutes
97540	Training in activities of daily living (self care skills and/or daily life management skills); initial 30 minutes, each visit
97541	each additional 15 minutes
97545	Work hardening/conditioning; initial 2 hours
97546	each additional hour

TESTS AND MEASUREMENTS

(For muscle testing, manual or electrical, joint range of motion, electromyography or nerve velocity determination, see 95831- 95904)

97000	Office visit, including one of the following tests or measurements, with report
	a. Orthotic "check-out"
	b. Prosthetic "check-out"
	c. Activities of daily living "check-out"; initial 30 minutes, each visit
97001	each additional 15 minutes
97720	Extremity testing for strenth, dexterity, or stamina; initial 30 minutes, each visit
97221	each additional 15 minutes
	(9740,97741 have been deleted. To report, see 97530,97531)
97752	Muscle testing with torque cruves during isometric and isokinetic exercise, mechanized or computerized evaluations with printout

OTHER PROCEDURES

97799	Unlisted physical medicine service or procedure
	(98900-98902 have been deleted. To report, use appropriate category and level of Evaluation and Management codes)
	(98910-98912 have been deleted. To report, see 99361-99362)
	(98920-98922 have been deleted. To report, see 99371-99373)

SPECIAL SERVICES AND REPORTS

The procedures with code numbers 99000 through 99090 provide the reporting physician with the means of identifying the completion of special reports and services that are an adjunct to the basic services rendered. The specific number assigned indicates the special circumstances under which a basic procedure is performed.

MISCELLANEOUS SERVICES

99000   Handling and/or conveyance of specimen for transfer from the physician's office to a laboratory

99001   Handling and/or conveyance of specimen for transer from the patient in other than a physician's office to a laboratory (distance may be indicated)

99002   Handling, conveyance, and/or any other service in connection with the implementation of an order involving devices (eg, designing, fitting, packaging, handling, delivery or mailing) when devices such as orthotics protectives, prosthetics are fabricated by an outside laboratory or shop but which items have been designed, and are to be fitted and adjusted by the attending physician.

(For routine collection of venous blood, use 36415)

Appendix 4
Normal Range of Motion, in Degrees
Following American Academy of Orthopedic Surgeons

JOINT	DEGREES	JOINT	DEGREES
Shoulder		Hip	
Flexion	180	Flexion	120
Extension	60	Extensiion	30
Abduction	180	Abduction	45
Internal			
Adduction	30	rotation	70
Internal			
External		rotation	45
rotation	90	External	
Horizontal		rotation	45
		adduction	135
Elbow		Knee	
Flexion	150	Flexion	135
Radioulnar		Ankle	
Pronation	80	Plantar Flexion	50
Supination	80	Dorsiflexion	20
Wrist		Subtalar joint	
Flexion	80	Inversion	35
Eversion	15		
Extension	70		
Radial			
deviation	20		
Ulnar			
deviation	30		

Appendix 5
Physical Therapy Modalities
(See also Abbreviation List in Appendix 1)

Term	Abbreviation
Ambulation training	AMB, AMBTR (see Gait)
Biofeedback	BFB, BFBK, Biofeed
Cervical traction	CTRX, CTX (see Traction)
Electrical stimulation therapy	EGS, HVGS, HVS, HVES, ES, ERX, Nueroprobe, high voltage galvanic, interferential, TENS, TNS
Electro diagnostic testing	EDX
Evaluation	EVAL
Exercise, therapeutic exer.	THEX, Ther ex, EX, E, AEX, PEX, AAEX
Functional capacity assess.	FCA
Functional capacity eval	FCE
Gait analysis	GA
Gait training	GT, GTr (see Ambulation)
Gonimoetrx (Range of motion)	GON
Hot packs	Hp
Ice, cold pack, cryotherapy	CRX, CRYO
Ice massage	IM
Infrared	IR
Initial Evaluation	IE
Joint mobilization	JM, Mob
Lumbar traction	LTX (see Traction)
Manual traction	MTX, MTRX (see Traction)
Manual Muscle Test	MMT, MT (strength test)
Massage	M, MG, Mas, MGE
Moist heat	MH
Moist Air Cabinet	mac

APPENDIX 5 PHYSICAL THERAPY MODALITIES

Myofascial release	MFR
Pelvic traction	PTRX, PTX (see Traction)
Range of Motion	ROM (See Gonimoetrix)
Re-evaluation	RE, Re-eval
Soft Tissue Mobilization (massage)	STM
Superficial heat	SH
Traction	TRX, TX, T
Ultrasound	US, U
Vasopneumatic devices	Jobst, compression, IPP, ICP (intermittent compression)
Whirlpool	WP, hydrotherapy, hydro
Work hardening	WH

*To obtain additional copies of **The Accident Game**...*
Fill in the coupon below

☐ **Yes,** please send me _____ copies of *The Accident Game*
    by Nathaniel Randolph at **$21.95** per copy.
Please add **$3.50** shipping and handling.
    ☐ I have enclosed a check for _____
    ☐ or charge my ☐ VISA ☐ MasterCard ☐ Amer Express

Credit Card Number _____
Exp. Date _____
Signature _____

Name _____
Address _____
City_____ State_____ Zip _____
Make check payable and send to:

Regal Publishing Corporation
321 New Albany Road, Moorestown, NJ 08057